TWINS AND HOMOSEXUALITY

GARLAND
GAY AND LESBIAN STUDIES
(VOL. 2)

GARLAND REFERENCE LIBRARY
OF SOCIAL SCIENCE
(VOL. 627)

GARLAND
GAY AND LESBIAN STUDIES

General Editor: Wayne R. Dynes

TWINS AND HOMOSEXUALITY
A Casebook

edited,
with an Introduction,
by
Geoff Puterbaugh

GARLAND PUBLISHING, INC. • NEW YORK & LONDON
1990

Library of Congress Cataloging-in-Publication Data

Twins and homosexuality: a casebook / edited, with an introduction by
Geoff Puterbaugh.
    p. cm. — (Garland reference library of social science; vol.
627. Garland gay and lesbian studies; vol. 2)
    Includes bibliographical references.
    ISBN 0-8240-6149-7 (alk. paper)
    1. Homosexuality. 2. Human genetics. 3. Twins—United States—
Case studies. 4. Gays—United States—Case studies.
I. Puterbaugh, Geoff. II. Series: Garland reference library of
social science; v. 627. III. Series: Garland reference library of
social science. Garland gay and lesbian studies; vol. 2.
HQ76.25.T78   1990
306.7'66—dc20   70720

                                        90-31756
                                              CIP

Printed on acid-free, 250-year-life paper
Manufactured in the United States of America

Acknowledgments

The editor would like to express his appreciaticn to the staff of the Stanford University Medical Library, and to all the courageous and inquiring authors whose work is reprinted herein. Special thanks go to Mr. Brian Decker, Dr. James Puterbaugh, Dr. Michael Ruse, Dr. Thomas Bouchard, and Dr. Wayne R. Dynes.

Grateful acknowledgment is made to the following for permission to reprint previously published material:

Williams and Wilkins, for Kallmann, F.: "Comparative Twin Study on the Genetic Aspects of Male Homosexuality," originally printed in *The Journal of Nervous and Mental Disease*, v. 115, pp. 283-98 (1952). Copyright 1952 Williams and Wilkins.

Williams and Wilkins, for Rainer, J.D., Mesnikoff, A., Kolb, L.C. and Carr, A.: "Homosexuality and Heterosexuality in Identical Twins," originally printed in *Psychosomatic Medicine*, v. 22, pp. 251-59 (1960). Copyright 1960 The American Psychosomatic Society.

Williams and Wilkins, for Klintworth, G.K.: "A Pair of Male Monozygotic Twins Discordant for Homosexuality," originally printed in *The Journal of Nervous and Mental Disease*, v. 135, pp. 113-25 (1962). Copyright 1962 Williams and Wilkins.

The American Medical Association, for Heston, L.L. and Shields, J.: "Homosexuality in Twins: A Family Study and a Registry Study," originally printed in *Archives of General Psychiatry*, v. 18, pp. 149-60 (1968). Copyright 1968 the American Medical Association.

The W. B. Saunders Company, for Zuger, B.: "Monozygotic Twins Discordant for Homosexuality: Report of a Pair and Significance of the Phenomenon," originally printed in *Comprehensive Psychiatry*, v. 17, pp. 661-69 (1976). Copyright 1976 Grune & Stratton.

Plenum Publishing Corporation, for McConaghy, N. and Blaszczynski. M.A.: "A Pair of Monozygotic Twins Discordant for Homosexuality: Sex-Dimorphic Behavior and Penile Volume Responses," originally printed in *Archives of Sexual Behavior*, v. 9, pp. 123-131 (1980). Copyright 1980 Plenum Publishing Corporation.

The Haworth Press, for Ruse, M.: "Are There Gay Genes? Sociobiology and Homosexuality," originally printed in *The Journal of*

Homosexuality, v. 6, pp. 5-34 (1981). Copyright 1981 The Haworth Press.
The Royal College of Psychiatrists, for Eckert, E.D., Bouchard, T.J., Bohlen, J. and Heston, L.L.: "Homosexuality in Monozygotic Twins Reared Apart," originally printed in *The British Journal of Psychiatry*, v. 148, pp. 421-425 (1985). Copyright 1985 The Royal College of Psychiatrists.

Table of Contents

Series Editor's Introduction

Wayne R. Dynes

In a half century our understanding of homosexual behavior has been transformed. During the 1940s psychiatric and medical approaches dominated the subject. When not simply characterized as social pathology, same-sex behavior still ranked as an aberration, something to be overcome. Hence the emphasis on therapy or "cures." Even then though change was in the air. The two Kinsey Reports of 1948 and 1953 not only revealed that the incidence of homosexual activity was much greater than previously thought but, by adopting neutral, nonjudgmental terminology, suggested that it lay within the normal range of human experience. This implicit assumption found confirmation in the research of a psychologist, Dr. Evelyn Hooker, who showed that using a random sample chosen from the general population − instead of the clinical sample routinely employed at that time − the performance of homosexual subjects on objective tests was indistinguishable from that of heterosexual ones. In retrospect, the most startling innovation was the founding of the homophile movement by Henry Hay and others in Los Angeles in 1950. Bedeviled by growing pains and the hostile atmosphere engendered by the McCarthyite trend, the movement evolved slowly. In 1969, however, in a climate of social ferment conditioned by the Civil Rights movement and opposition to the Vietnam War, the homophile movement turned a corner, a development symbolized by the Stonewall Riots in New York City.

The ensuing decades saw not only a torrent of publications − so many that bibliographers can scarcely keep up with them − but also a decisive shift in the center of gravity. Major works that could not be ignored now appeared under the authorship of open, proud gay men and lesbians. No longer was gay life described as a remote, exotic phenomenon, but directly by those who had actually experienced it and who had no hesitation in saying so. "They" yielded to "we." In an effort to correct previous distortions, some of these writings erred on the side of advocacy. Today, however, thanks to the mingling of many voices, a balance is being struck that is moving rapidly toward consensus.

Another shift was away from present-minded social science toward a new emphasis on cultural themes. Gay men and lesbians, it was increasingly recognized, had made immense contributions to the worlds of literature and drama, art and music, film and photography. Scholars could chart the role of the sexuality of many creative figures. Moreover, scrutiny of records from other cultures − Islam, China, and Japan, as well as a host of tribal cultures known from the field work of ethnographers − signaled the need for an understanding of same-sex behavior as a world-wide phenomenon. The new climate of acceptance revitalized the older approaches of sociology and psychology. Even those in the natural sciences, who, if they addressed the subject at all, had been hostile, reentered the arena with interesting though often still speculative contributions in the realms of sociobiology and constitutional biology.

Although the new research rightly seeks to overcome older negative approaches, questions of value persist. Survey of the history of the subject shows that in addition to ascertaining the facts of same-sex behavior and its cultural expression, it is essential to scrutinize attitudes toward it. All too often these have been disparaging − they have reflected facets of homophobia, the irrational dislike of sexual attraction between members of the same sex. While some scholars have contented themselves with tracing and recording the influence of these adversarial views, others have felt compelled to refute them. As in women's studies and black studies, this sense of a need to correct the record leads to a perceived departure from older ideals of dispassionate objectivity. Yet now that the more vehement expressions of outrage have passed, it is possible to see that a passion for justice is not incompatible with an objective search for truth.

Today the panorama of studies in the field is a rich one, and it is becoming richer still. In all likelihood, however, the subject of sexuality, linked as it is to so many other spheres of human aspiration, is inexhaustible.

The conception of this Series is deliberately pluralistic. Some volumes collect representative papers or articles together with critical commentary by the editor to bring a current issue into focus. Other books are substantial monographs reconsidering major aspects of the field. Intersecting with these two categories are research manuals, sometimes overtly bibliographic and sometimes more discursive, which serve as critical tools for advancing work in the field.

Geoff Puterbaugh is an independent scholar in northern California. A contributor to the *Encyclopedia of Homosexuality*, he has published many articles elsewhere on diverse aspects of our subject.

In a careful review of the evidence, scholars at the Alfred C. Kinsey Institute of Sex Research at Indiana University concluded that all environmental explanations of the origin of same-sex behavior had proven insufficient; therefore a new approach integrating biological perspectives is required (*11*).[1] What form this approach might take is as yet uncertain. But the evidence collected in this volume, which has been too long ignored, will be central to any new evaluation. The papers published here are controversial, to be sure; they are also indispensable.

---

1. Italic numbers in parentheses refer to items in the Combined Bibliography at the back of the book.

Introduction

Geoff Puterbaugh

Twins have long fascinated humanity.
Ever since the twin pairs of ancient myth (Castor and Pollux, the Gemini), observers have attempted to learn something from the twinning phenomenon. St. Augustine used the differing fates of twins as an argument against the claims of astrology. Some African tribes have viewed the twinning process as a ritual impurity, condemning both twins and their mother to death for an offense against tribal mores. Each advance in our knowledge about the science of human and animal reproduction has provided us with new tools and perspectives in our ongoing attempt to learn more about the universe and ourselves.

Men have always recognized the distinction between identical and fraternal twins. It is only quite recently, however, that our biological knowledge has enabled us to identify the cause of this distinction, and to establish a new branch of science (twin studies) with important ramifications for many other branches of science. Twin studies offer an extremely powerful tool for determining the differing forces of nature and nurture in shaping biological characteristics. Studies are ongoing in many different areas: hand selection, intelligence, criminality, and life expectancy are only the beginning of a long list. Some pioneering medical researchers also used this new scientific device to investigate the phenomenon of homosexuality, with some very surprising results.

This casebook has been compiled as an attempt to give these results a wider audience and to fill a gap in the published literature on homosexuality. The literature abounds with works which attempt to explain homosexuality as purely environmental in origin, while the alternative viewpoint (finding a scientific basis in twin studies) has been largely restricted to small articles in medical journals.

By its very nature, this casebook must be controversial. It could hardly be otherwise, since both homosexuality and the nature/nurture debate are contested issues in the late twentieth century. They are *fundamentally* contested issues, forcing the participants to confront basic questions of religion, philosophy, science, and popular culture; hard-won positions are not easily abandoned.

The articles gathered here may be of interest to the general reader in three different ways, which will be briefly discussed.

The Statistics

The first thread of interest is the significance of the statistics assembled by the various authors. To understand the statistics, it is necessary to assimilate the vocabulary of twin studies.

Monozygotic twins (or "identical twins") arise from one sperm fertilizing one egg. The fertilized egg later divides, resulting in two infants with a genetic complement usually assumed to be identical. (This assumption is brought into question below.)

Dizygotic twins (or "fraternal twins") arise from two eggs being fertilized by two sperm, and are generally no more closely related than any other two siblings. In fact, they are likely to be of different sexes.

Concordance is the degree to which two people share the same trait. John and Peter, not related, may be concordant for blue eyes, if they both have blue eyes. In twin studies, it is normal to cite concordance as a percentage: given 100 blue-eyed people, what is the concordance among the population at large, among siblings (brothers and sisters), among DZ (dizygotic) twins, and among MZ (monozygotic) twins?

The concordance rate for homosexuality among male MZ twins is the interesting number addressed by these studies.   If the theory of environmental causation were true, then one would expect no concordance for homosexuality at all; that is, homosexuals would appear at the basic Kinsey (*81*)[1] rate of 5 to 10 per cent of the male population.

But that is not the number which medical research gives us. If we add up all the pairs reported in these eight articles (including those summarized in Zuger (*173*) and in Heston and Shields (*61*)), we obtain the following totals: 65 pairs of male MZ twins, 50 of whom are concordant and 15 discordant.   This amounts to 77 per cent concordance among identical male twins. (Out of caution, this count excludes all females and all cases where schizophrenia was present.)

Furthermore, if we eliminate the recent spate of "freak" articles — articles published to study the puzzling case of discordant MZ twins, and

---

1. Italic numbers in parentheses refer to items in the Combined Bibliography at the back of the book.

which have a sample size of one discordant pair – we are left with 37 from Kallmann (*75*), 2 from Lange (*93*), 6 from Sanders (*134*), 5 from Habel (*52*), 4 from Heston and Shields (*61*), 1 from Farber (*34*), and 2 from Eckert and Bouchard (*32A*). This makes 57 pairs, 50 of whom are concordant, and 7 of whom are discordant. Analyzed in this way, the data would seem to suggest a concordance rate of about 88 per cent for homosexuality among male identical twins.

These calculations assume, somewhat carelessly, that there are no "non-admitters" present in these samples. We can safely assume that there are some: there are still people who will deny being left-handed when interrogated by official investigators. If people will deny a trivial item such as left-handedness, they will certainly deny something as emotionally charged as homosexuality. One example of the degree of lying that may be present in such investigations lies (unnoticed by any of our authors) in the bizarre results obtained by Koch (*83*). Koch claimed to have investigated 495 twin pairs, selected only as being "non-delinquent" and "non-psychiatric." He found one male homosexual and one female homosexual in a study population of almost 1,000 people. We must believe that Koch has overthrown the Kinsey report (reporting an incidence for homosexuality of approximately .02%, rather than 5-10%), or that all homosexuals are to be found in prisons and psychiatric wards, or that there was a great deal of "non-admitting" occurring.

The true concordance rate is not yet known. If it should prove to be as high as 80 or 90 per cent, then it would probably be enough to settle the nature/nurture debate. This conclusion may seem startling, since many people believe that even one discordant MZ pair must disprove the entire genetic case. Identical twins have identical genes: if they are discordant in regard to homosexuality, then clearly something else is at work.

The error in such reasoning lies in a faulty assumption, which is pointed out by two authors, Money and Klintworth (*112,82*): we already know that MZ twins are not necessarily identical in their gene complements. This has appeared in cases of MZ twins discordant for Down's syndrome and Turner's syndrome. Slight differences in the genotype can and do occur in ways which we are trying to determine (even Gregor Mendel has been rightly faulted for doctoring his pea studies to obtain exact ratios, where nature was not quite so exact). And this very slight difference may well be the mechanism which makes the concordance rate for male homosexuality less than 100%.

We must, given these figures for MZ twin pairs, compare them to the figures for DZ twins. The DZ twin pairs show no concordance at all for homosexuality, or a very slight concordance. In every case so far known to medical research, the DZ concordance rate has been so much lower than the MZ concordance rate that the DZ rate has generally been compared to the rate for siblings. And the DZ rate is consistent, whether the DZ twins were raised together or apart.

Since both DZ and MZ twins are usually raised together in the same environment, the champions of an environmental etiology are, rightly, puzzled.

In any case, the numbers from these twin studies are obviously much too high to allow any further credence to be given to theories of exclusively environmental causation.

There are some important addenda and caveats for any general hypothesis that all cases of true homosexual orientation are genetically caused. First, it does not establish a genetic foundation for every case of homosexual behavior. Since time immemorial, men have performed homosexual acts in special environments such as prisons and naval vessels, where women were unavailable. For an equally long time, other men have performed homosexual acts in exchange for money or other favors. Male prostitution has a pedigree as ancient as its female counterpart.

Second, we do not find any particular type of homosexuality predominating in the twin studies. The various categories of male homosexuality (effeminate men, pederasts, loving comrades, overtly masculine homosexuals, and so on) are all represented here.

A final finding of general interest is that all the male MZ twins raised together emphatically denied any sexual interest in their co-twins at any time in their lives. This presents a strong contrast to the male MZ twins raised apart, where such attraction was reported by all the homosexual males, one pair even becoming lovers at the age of 24. This is one more bit of statistical evidence for what appears to be a near-universal pattern of incest-avoidance: people seem to have no sexual interest in the other children they were raised with, whether or not related by blood.

The Received Wisdom

The second thread of interest in these articles falls into the category of the "sociology of knowledge," or the study of "received ideas." Kallmann published his classic study (75) in 1952, and almost no one listened to him. In 1952, the American followers of psychiatry were beginning their days of glory, Freudianism and environmental determinism were the order of the day, and Kallmann was simply ignored.

If he was not ignored, he was refuted. Our second article, by Rainer *et al.* (*128*), is an attempt to make Kallmann irrelevant by finding (and publishing) one discordant pair. As we have already seen, this finding is an event of no particular importance, but, in 1960, it was evidence that psychiatry was strongly enough entrenched to feel that this rather feeble effort was sufficient to keep the "enemy" silenced, and ignored. (It is also interesting to read the article carefully, and wonder if this pair is truly discordant. The authors were "cure therapists," and the brothers are perhaps only dissimilar in their desire to present a "heterosexual façade.")

To the present day, many people who consider themselves educated find the idea of a genetic cause for homosexuality unworthy of serious discussion, because they "know" that all sexual behavior is learned. But a growing number of people are willing to reconsider the matter, and that is due to recent political and historical events as much as any "scientific breakthrough."

For one thing, homosexuality was decriminalized in most major areas of the United States, and in England and Germany as well. This was a decisive legal victory, which permanently altered the lives of male homosexuals (and lesbians as well, to a lesser extent).

Another major advance was the decision that homosexuality was not a mental illness. Although this medical decision was arrived at by a process of voting (surely an odd method), it too had a major impact on public thinking.

And of course there was Stonewall, after which the gay liberation movement burst into action in all the industrialized nations around the globe.

Simultaneously with this process, psychiatry was going into a decline. Dr. Bieber's book, *Homosexuality* (*14*), intended to be the triumphant final statement on the subject, proved over time to be so faulty in procedures and methodologies that it is no longer cited by medical professionals. C. A. Tripp did yeoman service in exposing Bieber's many errors in his own *The Homosexual Matrix* (*155*), an important text of the 1970's, which became a bible for many gay men.

But scholars of homosexuality became most frustrated with the appearance of the Kinsey Institute's *Sexual Preference* in 1981 (*11*). This massive study of homosexual men examined all the leading environmental theories, and found no support for any of them. Absent fathers, over-loving mothers, birth order, the labeling theory − all of these beloved theories were suddenly revealed to be empty of any scientific or predictive value.[2] This opened the door for a serious discussion of the causes of homosexual orientation, and thus permitted a re-examination of the medical texts gathered in this casebook. And, as of this writing, it is the "received wisdom" that the cause of homosexuality is unknown, but (although it is unknown) it is somehow known that it is caused by genetics and the environment together.

This may be the case, and the reader will reach his own decision based on the evidence and his own knowledge. It is possible, however, that the current "received wisdom" merely represents a midpoint between the old idea that the etiology of homosexuality was entirely environmental, and a future idea that homosexuality is nothing more than a common and benign genetic variation.

The Medical Question

The third thread of interest in these articles is, for many gay men, another subtext: is the "disease" under discussion here "homosexuality," or is it rather "homophobia"? Is either of these phenomena properly designated a "disease," presumably to be treated by medical doctors? Or are we really talking about "things I don't happen to like"?

It is certainly disturbing (and melancholy) to find the opening article by Kallmann printed in the *Journal of Nervous and Mental Disease*. Kallmann surely regarded himself as an impartial scientist, and yet his article (which was to assume such great importance for gay men) is a noteworthy example of the language of pejoration being used in the broadest and least subtle of ways. Virtually every condemnatory category available is used: "deviant," "intrinsically maladjusted," "aberrant," "gloomy," "immature," "disturbed," "fixated" and more make it clear that Kallmann never questioned that he was dealing with a disease, or, as he finally put it, with an "alternative minus variant." The fact that he was also dealing with an illegal form of behavior he mentions casually, in noting that he cannot put forward too many details because his homosexual citizens are "still subject to the laws of the State of New York."

Yet it never seems to occur to Kallmann that the prevailing assumptions of the time (that homosexuality is both a mental disease

---

2. Note that Michael Ruse's article, "Are There Gay Genes?" – reprinted here – appeared in the same year (1981) and therefore, unfortunately, gives some of these discredited theories (such as birth order) more credence than they appear to deserve.

and a crime, as well as a mortal sin) might have had some role in explaining the "gloominess" of his subjects. It is only in the last two decades that some judicious minds have begun questioning whether a homophobia as thorough and vicious as Kallmann's is a social benefit, especially in a land where all men are declared to be free and equal in the pursuit of life, liberty, and happiness.

And that is the third thread which can be seen developing in these articles. By the time of Heston and Shields, there is already much less pejoration and even some care to notice that schizophrenia and homosexuality are not concordant — that, whatever homosexuality may or may not be, it is not concordant with "real mental illness."

By the time we reach the last article in the book, such homophobic language is almost entirely gone, and the analysis is the most cautious and detached.

This development can only be praised, since the entire field of twin studies and homosexuality has been perturbed and distorted by ideological passions and medical empire-building for so many years. In the decades to come, we may hope to see more studies of twins raised apart, a greater emphasis on longitudinal twin studies, a greater mass of data, and certainly more research into the startling possibility (brought out by Eckert *et al.* in the present volume) that lesbianism may have an etiology entirely different from that of male homosexuality.

Twins and Homosexuality

Comparative Twin Study
on the Genetic Aspects
of Male Homosexuality[1]

Franz J. Kallmann, M.D.

When the objectives of a combined twin and sibship study of overt homosexuality in the adult male were formulated by us in 1947, we were prepared for a series of codified sensitivities to both deviant forms of sex behavior and genetically controlled imperfections in the existence of modern man. Nevertheless, we were confident that the experience gained in previous population surveys of a similar magnitude would prove to be useful. We soon discovered, however, that we had been rather inexpert, or overly optimistic, or possibly both.

We know now that it is quite inadvisable to underrate the particular methodologic difficulties, which are inherent in a search for verifiable data concerning the cultural backgrounds and sex experiences of a series of *distrusting* research subjects, or to overrate the durability of a professed spirit of co-operation on the part of social agencies which seem eager to act as secret guardians of an intrinsically maladjusted group of our society. In fact, we are ready to concede at this point that an investigation of the sexual habits and self-protective devices of an ostracized class of people and their family relations is not a promising field of exploration for research workers who are in any way concerned about their conventional peace of mind. Psychiatrically it has been

1. This report was presented at the combined meeting of the New York Neurological Society and the Section of Neurology and Psychiatry of the New York Academy of Medicine on January 15, 1951, and dealt with the progress of an investigation, which was supported by a grant from the Committee for Research in Problems of Sex, National Research Council.
From the Department of Medical Genetics of the New York State Psychiatric Institute, Columbia University, New York, N. Y.

4 *Twins and Homosexuality: A Casebook*

interesting to confirm, however, that the problems and attitudes of a sexually aberrant group look less wholesome in the twilight of gloomy hiding places than they do from the perspective of an ornamental desk or from a comfortable therapeutic couch.

Procedurally it is especially impedient in a twin family study of this kind that the road from the point of procuring the name and recorded history of an apparently homosexual twin to the establishment of a formal acquaintance with the given person or his relatives is an incredibly long, rugged, and sometimes perilous one. The subjects are astute in disguising their identities, shifting whereabouts and family connections. They usually live far from their families, and they are rarely able or willing to discuss more than their personal histories. In addition, most of them are unavailable for laboratory tests, since they insist that meetings be arranged in accordance with their habits of precaution, that is, at neutral meeting places.

In view of these difficulties it was evident from the beginning that the *twin study method* would be technically much too cumbersome a procedure to warrant its application for the sole purpose of demonstrating the basic genetic origin of both structural and functional aspects of every type of sex behavior. Regardless of whether the term "homosexuality" is applied to the formation of all, or only to the practice of overt, sexual relations between individuals of the same sex (*81*), it has always been clear that neither the quality nor the object of a person's sexual striving can possibly undergo a habitual fixation without the pre-existence of the organic components of sexuality, which may sometimes fail to be integrated into a mature form of sex behavior.

This statement does not mean, of course, that sex-controlling genes are suspected genetically of being able to determine the final choice of a sex partner. For similar reasons, no gene is assumed to produce a special preference for saccharine, even if it may be held responsible for a certain type of biochemical dysfunction resulting in the symptomology of diabetes mellitus. It is rather unnecessary, therefore, to over-stress the nonexistence of "inheritable qualities in the structurization of the sex potentiality that would direct a person either away from a member of the same sex or toward the opposite sex" (*66*).

Although gonadal hormones are known to be essential for the activation and gradual differentiation of maturational processes, they are only the tools, with which the genetic constitution of an organism directs its sexual development from a morphologically neutral embryonic stage to the functional responsiveness of adult sex adjustment. Originally, all the developmental potentialities of one or the other sex are determined by the chromosomal make-up of the gametes. The starting point for any differentiation of maturational processes depends on whether a sperm bearing a paternal grandmother's X-chromosome or a sperm bearing the grandfather's Y-chromosome unites with the ovum. Following fertilization, the process of mitosis takes care of providing every cell of the developing embryo and ultimate adult with the original XX- or XY-constitution of the fertilized ovum (*149*).

As a rule, the balance established between the sex-controlling effect of one or two X-chromosomes and that of the other chromosomes operates with a sufficient margin of safety to preclude intersexual development, that is, imperfect determination of one or the other sex due to a disturbed balance of female and male genetic tendencies. However, if a breakdown in the usual process of clearly alternative differentiation between the sexes occurs, the maturational effect of one or the other of the opposing sex genes may be weakened precariously. Such an organic disarrangement is apt to lead to a variety of intersexual deviations, interfering with full integration of the ordinary patterns of sexual maturation.

According to psychodynamic theories of sociologic or psychoanalytic orientation, a possible causal relationship between an organically disarranged sex constitution and a tendency to overt homosexuality in the adult can be safely disregarded. A certain degree of sexual feeling toward one's own sex is assumed to remain a residual trait in every person, as the result of what is originally considered to be a complete freedom of choice. Subsequent preference for predominantly homosexual patterns is believed to be a product of individual learning and experience (*16,60,97,105*). Final adherence to homosexual outlets in men is ascribed either to the conditioning compulsiveness of social ostracism with respect to common "physiologic" deviations from the moral code of our society (*66,81*) or to traumatized regression and fixation to immature levels of sexuality (*2,13,35*). In line with the latter concept, inversive anxiety may be aroused by competitiveness in the oedipal situation and is apt to result in one of two possible patterns of response, namely, in seductive submission to the parental rival or in erotized identification with the mother.

In addition, the specific psychodynamic significance of certain personality deviations has been emphasized by a group of psychiatrically experienced investigators, especially by Bychowski, Hoch, and Rado (*66*). The evidence of such special psychopathologic phenomena in homosexual men is said to include general personality distortion with a prevalence of schizoid or "schizo-sexual" disorganization as well as the "obsessive" feature of insistence on pregenital or paragenital gratification patterns. Surprisingly, Kinsey (*81*) generally disfavors any explanation of male homosexuality which would imply the possibility of "pan-sexuality" in the sense of polymorphic-perverse stages in psychosexual development. In relation to this point, the element of surprise stems from the fact that Kinsey does not seem to be entirely opposed to a consideration of genetic factors as a potential source of variations in sexual responsiveness, at least indirectly through inheritance of certain physical characteristics or behavioral qualities "which may help to develop human personality."

Otherwise, only a few contemporary investigators (*10,29,41,44,63*) have shown an inclination to give cautious support to a *genetic theory* of male homosexuality as originally suggested by Krafft-Ebing (*86*). In the opinion of Henderson and Gillespie (*59*), for instance, the probability of a primary constitutional basis in some apparently conditioned types of male homosexuality is indicated not only by the frequency of physical characteristics which, like the horizontal pubic hair pattern, belong to the female sex, but also by the unusual number of homosexual men displaying "special artistic ability." *Familial* occurrence, notably in brothers, is said by Hirschfeld (*63*) to have been observed in 35 per cent of homosexual males, and concordance as to overt homosexuality has been reported by three investigators (*63,134,148*) in a total of 14 male twin pairs classified as monozygotic.   Goldschmidt's theory of an intersexual origin of certain forms of human homosexuality is known to have been formulated on the basis of experiments conducted with gypsy moths (*45*). The main support for the application of this theory in man has come from the observation made by Lang (*87,88,89,90,91,92*) as well as by Jensch (*73,74*), that the sex ratio among the siblings of male homosexuals seems to deviate sharply from ordinary expectation.

However, the *statistical* adequacy of these studies has been criticized by both Koller (*85*) and Darke (*25,25A*). Equal validity is probably attached to Kinsey's statement that an increase in the homosexuality rates for the blood relatives of homosexuals has never been substantiated by means of statistically satisfactory investigations. It is evident, too, that if some homosexual men are assumed to be genetically female although phenotypically male intersexes without a Y-chromosome, their children should all be female.   It would be preferable, therefore, to ascertain a significant deviation of the expected sex ratio in relation to the *offspring* rather than the siblings of homosexual males. In fact, Slater (*141*) is correct in stressing that the most conclusive test of the intersexuality theory would be procured by a *cytologic* examination of chromosomal biopsy material, which should show the lack of a Y-chromosome in intersexes with a known homosexual history.   In the absence of such cytologic data, it is fair to admit that the question of the possible significance of genetic mechanisms in the development of overt homosexuality may still be regarded as entirely unsettled.

Taking notice of this generally unsatisfactory state of information about the genetic aspects of adult homosexual behavior, explained at least in part by the previously described methodologic difficulties, our investigative plan aimed at a simultaneous and concentric attack from several directions.   The frontal approach was based on the collection of an unselected and statistically representative sample of predominantly or exclusively homosexual *twin index cases* over age 20 or, preferably, over age 30.   The search for potential index cases was organized not only with the aid of psychiatric, correctional and charitable agencies, but also through direct contacts with the clandestine homosexual world.   In addition, our procedure was arranged in such a manner as to provide verified clinical, social, and, whenever possible, cytologic data for graduated sex ratings of the index cases as well as their co-twins, brothers, and fathers, and for an adequately controlled determination of the sex ratio among the siblings and children of the index cases.   However, some of these goals remained beyond reach within the given limits of time and organizational range, since scientific objectives and criteria in investigations of sexual deviations are much easier to devise than to attain in actual practice.

For instance, sex classifications can be made only of those children who have been born to homosexual subjects, but the actual size of this birth rate will be found to be inversely related to the rigidity of the criteria applied in the collection of homosexual index cases.   If the present report is limited to a consecutive series of plainly homosexual twin index cases with fully recorded sex and family histories, this series provides verified evidence only of a total of 11 marriages contracted by an adult sample of 85 men with a homosexuality rating of group 3 or higher (Kinsey's scale).   Most of these marriages lasted no longer than a few months, and only three of them were fertile, resulting in a total fertility quota of five children, three boys and two girls.   Unfortunately, in no instance has it been possible to confirm the paternity of the legal fathers beyond reasonable doubt.

The data on the sex histories of the parents and siblings of the index cases are still insufficient and have not been included in this preliminary analysis.   It may be mentioned, however, that of the 85 *fathers* only one is known at present to have had a history of overt homosexual behavior, in addition to several convictions for pedophilic acts.

The sex distribution of the 187 *siblings* of the index cases is recorded in Table I and has been arranged in such a manner that the sex ratios observed can be compared with the results of the surveys of both Lang (*87,88,89,90,91,92*) and Darke (*25,25A*). In our sample, notable deviations from the expected ratio (106 males : 100 females) appear only in the sibships of those index cases, who are over age 25 (130.8) or not exclusively homosexual (169.6). According to Kinsey's scheme (*81*), individuals in groups 3 and 4 stand midway on the heterosexual-homosexual scale or still maintain a fair amount of heterosexual activity. Evidently, if it can be confirmed by larger samples that the sharpest deviation from the expected sex ratio occurs in the sibships of homosexual men showing an indiscriminately promiscuous or polymorphic type of sex behavior, the biologic meaning of this finding would be of definite significance.

TABLE I. - Sex Ratio in the Sibships of Male Homosexuals

		Homosexual Males	Siblings of Index Cases			Probability	
Age and Sex Rating		Number of Index Cases	Brothers	Sisters	Sex Ratio* (to 100 females)	t	x^2
Lang's Study	Under 26	516	778	687	113.2	1.23	1.51
	Over 25	499	956	745	128.3	3.92**	15.07**
	Total	1,015	1,734	1,432	121.1	3.67**	13.54**
Darke's Study	Under 26	44	82	67	122.4	.88	.74
	Over 25	56	96	101	95.0	.80	.62
	Total	100	178	168	106.0	.04	.00
Present Study	Under 26	17	19	18	105.6	.01	.00
	Over 25	68	85	65	130.8	1.26	1.59
	Groups 5 & 6	60	65	60	108.3	.11	.02
	Groups 3 & 4	25	39	23	169.6	1.80	3.25
	Total	85	104	83	125.3	1.14	1.27

* Expected sex ratio: 106 males : 100 females
** Significant

The total sibship sex ratio in our sample[2] is 125:100, approximating the one observed by Lang (121:100). However, contrary to Lang's figures, which are statistically significant at the .01 level for the older and the total groups of his study, the deviations in our proportionally smaller sample of "twin" index cases fail to reach the level of statistical significance with respect to both t and chi-square (x^2) values.

If the degree of significance in the present sample is computed for the subgroup with the largest value of t, that is, for the sibships of groups 3 and 4, t equals 1.80.

$$Where\ t = \frac{P-p}{\sigma p} ,$$

$$P = \frac{Observed\ number\ of\ male\ siblings}{total\ number\ of\ siblings\ (N)} ,$$

$$p = \frac{106}{206} = .515,\ q = 1 - .515 = .485,$$

$$\sigma p = \sqrt{\frac{pq}{N}} = \sqrt{\frac{(.515)(.485)}{N}}$$

In this instance, therefore, t would have to be 2.07 at the .05 level of confidence and 2.81 at the .01 level in order to be statistically significant. The corresponding x^2 values for the sample would have to be 3.84 at the .05 level, and 6.63 at the .01 level.

$$Where\ X_1 = Number\ of\ male\ siblings,$$

$$m_1 = (Total\ number\ of\ siblings)\ (.515),$$

$$X_2 = Number\ of\ female\ siblings,$$

$$m_2 = (Total\ number\ of\ siblings)\ (.485),$$

$$\chi^2 = \frac{(X_1 - m_1)^2}{m_1} + \frac{(X_2 - m_2)^2}{m_2}$$

It may be noted that the t and x^2 values show either the same lack of significance or an equally insufficient degree of significance in the

2. It is a pleasure to acknowledge not only the helpful co-operation extended by many official agencies, especially the New York State Department of Correction and Mental Hygiene, the New York State Division of Parole, the Probation Division of the New York City Magistrates' Court and the New York City Department of Correction, but also the valuable assistance rendered by members of our departmental research staff in the difficult investigative tasks of the survey (G.A. Colom, J.J. Danek, A. Falek, M. Gelfarb, K. Planasky, W.H. Shaw, J.A. Tieman, W. Wolfson) as well as in the statistical analysis of the collected data (G. Freedman).

present study. It will be necessary, therefore, to re-examine the question as to the presence or absence of consistent deviations in the sex ratio of homosexual index sibships on the basis of our numerically larger sample of single-born index cases.

More explicit are the comparative data in Table II, pertaining to the sex classifications of the *twin index pairs* themselves. Of 45 homosexual twin subjects in the *dizygotic* group, a total of 26 index cases had a twin brother who survived beyond the age of 18 years and was available for a complete investigation of his sex history. In this group, over one half (57.7 per cent) of the co-twins of distinctly homosexual subjects revealed no evidence of overt homosexual experiences after the onset of adolescence. According to whether the *dizygotic concordance rate* for homosexual behavior are related only to homosexuality ratings 5-6 or to the total range 1-6, they amount to 11.5 per cent or to 42.3 per cent, respectively, and are slightly higher than Kinsey's rates of 10 per cent and 37 per cent for the total male population, although the percentages obtained in the present study may be acceptable only as minimum figures.

TABLE II. - Gradations of Overt Homosexuality (Kinsey's Rating Scale) in the Co-Twins of 85 Male Homosexuals

Twin Index Cases				One-Egg Co-Twins						Two-Egg Co-Twins					
Sex Classification	Age	Zygocity One-Egg	Zygocity Two-Egg	6	5	4	3	2,1,0	Unclassified ed	6,5	4,3	2	1	0	Unclassified ed*
6	18-25	2	2	2	-	-	-	-	-	1	1	-	-	-	-
	26-35	10	8	8	1	-	-	-	1	-	-	-	2	1	5
	Over 35	8	9	6	2	-	-	-	-	-	-	-	3	4	2
5	18-25	3	3	-	1	-	1	-	1	-	-	-	-	2	1
	26-35	2	3	1	-	-	1	-	-	-	-	-	-	1	2
	Over 35	5	5	2	2	1	-	-	-	-	-	-	1	2	2
4	18-25	-	3	-	-	-	-	-	-	1	-	-	-	-	2
	26-35	2	3	-	-	2	-	-	-	1	-	-	-	1	1
	Over 35	3	3	-	1	-	2	-	-	-	-	-	-	1	2
3	18-25	2	2	-	1	-	-	-	1	-	-	-	-	1	1
	26-35	1	1	-	1	-	-	-	-	-	-	-	1	-	-
	Over 35	2	3	-	2	-	-	-	-	-	-	-	-	2	1
Total Number		40	45	19	9	5	4	0	3	1	2	1	7	15	19

* Including 14 females and 5 unclassified males (deceased or otherwise unavailable).

On the basis of Kinsey's observations, 37 per cent of all males admit to at least some overt homosexual experience between adolescence and old age, while 10 per cent may be expected to be more or less exclusively homosexual (groups 5 and 6) for at least three years between the ages of 16 and 55. It may be borne in mind, however, that Kinsey's data on overt homosexuality apply to men distinguished by their willingness to co-operate with an investigation of ordinary *sex* behavior, and that the results of the present study pertain to the twin partners of index cases with a known history of homosexual experiences, that is, to men who had merely been requested to co-operate with the investigative aims of a *twin* study. It seems reasonable to conclude, therefore, that the tendency to overt homosexuality in adulthood is *moderately increased* in men who are the brothers (dizygotic twin partners) of predominantly or exclusively homosexual index cases.

A completely different situation is encountered in that group of 40 index pairs classified as *monozygotic*. This series does not include a single co-twin of an overtly homosexual person standing at least midway on the homosexuality scale, who is classifiable either as entirely heterosexual or as homosexual below group 3. The majority of one-egg pairs not only are fully *concordant* as to the overt practice and quantitative rating of their aberrant sex pattern, but they even tend to be *very similar* in both the part taken in their individual sex activities and the visible extent of feminized appearance and behavior displayed by some of them.

It also seems significant that most of these index pairs assert to have developed their sexual tendencies *independently* and often *far apart* from each other, and that all of them deny categorically any history of mutuality in overt sex relations. The ostensible aversion to such an incestuous relationship is expressed even by those twin subjects who admit pre-adolescent sex play with a sister. In fact, the sexual taboo between homosexual twin brothers is generally carried so far that they disclaim not only the possibility of having had the same sex partner, but also that of being familiar with any intimate details of the co-twin's sex life. Apparently, the habitual secretiveness of homosexual men is maintained even by twin brothers who live together and have formed an entity in many other respects.

Psychiatrically it is of interest to note that apart from the striking similarity in sexual patterns, six of the index cases classified as monozygotic and concordant as to overt homosexuality have also been concordant with respect to schizophrenic episodes either before or after the manifestation of their homosexual tendencies. This group includes a pair of World War II veterans who, in addition to their histories of concordance as to homosexuality and schizophrenia, ended their lives by suicide in different ways (drowning and gas) and at different times (at the ages of 25 and 29, respectively) and thus became the first set of twins in whom this unusual occurrence has been authentically observed in modern times (79).

Because of the general significance of this monozygotic pair of schizophrenic twin brothers concordant as to homosexuality and death by self-destruction, it may be mentioned that the U. twins were of English-German descent, from a thrifty middleclass family, and the only sons of their parents (they had an older sister). Their early lives were uneventful, except for the fact that one of them (the second with respect to delivery and suicide) required plastic surgery on account of a disfiguring facial birth injury (left lower jaw) which seems to have been responsible for a certain retardation in physical and mental development. In 1942, the twins entered different branches of the Armed Services from different universities, in spite of their histories of overt homosexual behavior and although the disfigured twin had been a conscientious objector. Within less than a year, they developed similar schizophrenic symptoms in different theaters of war, but at practically the same time. Following shock treatment in different hospitals, they were unable to readjust themselves to civilian life, apparently because they were equally defective in their personalities and equally unmanageable in their tendencies to periodic vagabondism. The suicides were committed before and after the death of the mother (one at home, the other away from home) and were ascribed to fear of readmission to a mental hospital. In this tragic manner, the U. twins served to confirm our recently expressed opinion that "the suicides of two twin partners are apt to occur, but will only be observed by chance (not directly related to one another even under similar conditions of unfavorable family background, social frustration, or emotional maladjustment) and, therefore, will be extremely rare" (79). The photographs of the pair are withheld upon the request of the twins' father.[3]

---

3. None of the original photographs have been reprinted here. The three photographs in the original article showed three pairs of identical twins. Figure 1 (the J. twins) is a full front view of two middle-aged men, identically dressed in long-sleeved shirts and slacks. Figure 2 (the O. twins) shows head-and-shoulders of two middle-aged men in coat and tie, smiling. Figure 3 (the K. twins) shows full front view of two men posed as entertainers, with full suit and tie, hands in suit-coat pocket and elbows protruding, with the right leg crossed over the left, resting on the toe. All of the photos are

Of the remaining subjects in the group of monozygotic twins concordant as to homosexuality, at least 22 index cases are classifiable as definitely schizoid, severely unstable with obsessive-compulsive features, or excessively alcoholic. Evidence of transvestism has been observed in 7 cases of the total sample. Altogether, only 10 twin subjects of the monozygotic series and 18 subjects of the entire sample have been diagnosed as sufficiently adjusted, both emotionally and socially.

The photographs of three concordant one-egg pairs are shown in Figs. 1 - 3, to illustrate the different types of homosexual behavior in this series. The J. twins (Fig. 1), who traveled as stewards all over the world, were sturdy and masculine in both their appearance and sex activities. The O. twins (Fig. 2) were heavy drinking night club entertainers, who specialized as female impersonators and belonged to the entirely passive type of homosexual. The K. twins (Fig. 3) earned their living as models and entertainers until their careers were ended by excessive alcoholism. In this pair, one twin introduced the other to some of his homosexual friends of either variety. Further clinical or photographic data cannot be revealed, since most of the twin index cases of this survey are still subject to the laws of the State of New York.

In an attempt to fit the *palpable results* of this study into a sufficiently broad and genetically sound concept of male homosexuality, it seems advisable to view overt homosexual behavior in the adult male as an *alternative minus variant* in the integrative process of psychosexual maturation rather than as a pathognomonically determinative expression of a codifiable entity of behavioral immaturity. Apparently, the interactions between the biologic components of sexual maturation and the adjustive phenomena of personality development form such a central and inseparable interrelationship that fractional deviations in the psychosomatic integration of the sex function from its pregenital elements to genital maturity may dislocate the axis, around which the organization of the personality takes place.

On the whole, the adaptational equilibrium between the potentialities of organic sex differentiation and the consequent patterns of psychosexual behavior seems to be so labile that the attainment of a maturational balance may be disarranged at different developmental stages and by a variety of disturbing mechanisms. The range of such a *multiple causation* of inversive tendencies apparently extends from an unbalanced effect of opposing sex genes to the equivalent of compulsive rigidity in a schizoid personality structure. From a genetic standpoint,

---

disfigured by a thick black line drawn across the men's eyes, a device of the 1950's to attempt to preserve the anonymity of a subject while publishing a photograph of him.

this range would be comparable to the extent of developmental possibilities in relation to left-handedness which, as an alternative variant in the integration of handedness, is in a predominantly right-handed human world what adult homosexuality is in the sexually reproductive human species. As to left-handedness, however, few investigators claim that a genetically controlled basis or a certain unilateral use of the function of the left hand is precluded by a conditioned dexterity of the right hand, while analogous assumptions with respect to homosexual behavior are bitterly contended.

The disintegrative impact of those factors, which may lead to a psychosexual incapacity rather than to an optional dislike for true love attachments on a mature heterosexual level, clearly expresses itself in a virtually complete degree of concordance as to overt male homosexuality in a sample of *one-egg* twins. It is indicated by this finding that two males who are very similar in both the genotypical and the phenotypical aspects of their personality developments are much more likely than dizygotic twin brothers or ordinary siblings to be alike in those specific vulnerabilities which favor a trend toward fixation or regression to immature levels of sexuality. The infeasibility of the old theory (*136*), which associated a narcissistic preference for a homosexual object choice with a striking physical resemblance between homosexual partners, is demonstrated by a complete *lack of mutuality* in the sex histories of homosexual twin brothers.

If our concordance rates for *dizygotic* index pairs and Kinsey's homosexuality ratings for the total male population are statistically comparable, their rather close correspondence weakens the significance of some popular etiologic concepts of male homosexuality. Apart from militating against the probability of a *special genetic factor*, capable of turning the psychosexual integration of the adult male into an overt homosexual pattern, the observation of an only moderately increased concordance rate of overt homosexuality in genetically dissimilar twin brothers raised together plainly diminishes the plausibility of explanations which overstress the importance of such precipitating or perpetuating factors as social ostracism, incompetence of a particular parent, or other potentially traumatizing experiences arising from the effect of uncontrolled imperfections in the structure of modern human societies. Of course, the general conclusion that habitual predominance of a homosexual behavior pattern results from disturbing experiences only in a *limited* number of persons, by no means minimizes the psychodynamic significance of these constellational factors in potentially vulnerable individuals.

The *intersexuality* theory or, more precisely, a genetically oriented *"imbalance"* theory is still based on statistically insufficient and ctyologically unconfirmed evidence, but it has not been eliminated as a possible explanation for certain groups of male homosexuals. The principle of a disturbed balance between male and female genetic tendencies in these cases would not even be invalidated by the observation that some homosexual men have both a Y-chromosome and children who are boys. It is conceivable that phenotypically male homosexuals, who may be the product of an intersexual imbalance, are generally the ones distinguished by *infertility*.

Beyond question, the eventual exploration of the biologic components of male homosexuality will not be possible without the careful planning and a liberal financial support for more basic research, the execution of which has been shown by our experiences to be extremely difficult. It is also undeniable that the *urgency* of such additional work with respect to the genetic aspects of homosexual behavior is underscored by the ominous fact that adult homosexuality continues to be an inexhaustible source of unhappiness, discontent, and a distorted sense of human values.

Summary

1. In a consecutive series of 85 predominantly or exclusively homosexual male twin index cases, concordance as to the overt practice and quantitative rating of homosexual behavior after adolescence has been observed in all of the monozygotic index pairs (40). While many of the concordant twin partners claim to have developed their often very similar sexual pattern independently and far apart from each other, all of them deny any history of mutuality in overt sex relations. It does not seem justified, therefore, to explain a "narcissistic preference for a homosexual object choice" on the basis of a striking physical resemblance between homosexual partners.

2. Apparently, only two males who are similar in both the genotypical and the developmental aspects of sexual maturation and personality integration are also apt to be alike in those specific vulnerabilities favoring a trend toward fixation or regression to immature levels of sexuality. The most plausible explanation of this finding is that the axis, around which the organization of personality and sex function take place, is so easily dislocated that the attainment of a maturational balance may be disarranged at different developmental stages and by a variety of disturbing mechanisms, the range of which may extend from an unbalanced effect of opposing sex genes to the equivalent of

compulsive rigidity in a schizoid personality structure. From a genetic standpoint, this multiple causation of overt homosexual behavior in the adult male as an alternative minus variant in the integrative process of psychosexual maturation is comparable to that of left-handedness in a predominantly right-handed world.

3. In the dizygotic group of index pairs, over one half of the co-twins of distinctly homosexual subjects yield no evidence of overt homosexuality. According to whether the dizygotic concordance rates are related to homosexuality ratings 5-6 or 1-6, they vary from 11.5 per cent to 42.3 per cent and are only slightly in excess of Kinsey's ratings for the total male population. This finding weakens the significance of explanations which overstress such precipitating or perpetuating factors as social ostracism or parental incompetence in the etiology of adult homosexuality.

4. The total fertility quota of the index cases (11 marriages) consists of 3 boys and 2 girls. The sex ratio among the 187 siblings of the index cases (125:100) deviates from ordinary expectation, but the deviation fails to reach the level of statistical significance, underscoring the need for more extensive data with respect to a genetically oriented "imbalance" theory of male homosexuality.

Homosexuality and Heterosexuality in Identical Twins[1]

J. D. Rainer, M.D., A. Mesnikoff, M.D.,
L. C. Kolb, M.D., and A. Carr, Ph.D.

The value of the twin study method has been demonstrated as a means of approaching the study of genetic determinations of the mental disorders. Kallmann's (127) studies, which disclosed the concordant occurrence of the schizophrenic reaction in a large series of one-egg twins as contrasted to the low concordance in two-egg twins and siblings, are a model example of this type of investigation.

Such studies have concerned themselves largely with the concordance of similar types of personality organization. In its large context the following presentation represents the initial step in a series of studies directed to examining those factors responsible for the divergent development of behavioral traits in identical twins. It utilizes a variation of the co-twin control method which consists in observing selected pairs of one-egg twins whose physiological reactions and psychological adaptations may be compared under different life conditions. The present design is arranged to examine identical twin pairs with divergent development using current physical and biological (biochemical and tissue examinations), and psychological and historical (psychoanalytical) techniques and family studies for their possible correlations with dissimilarities in a given behavioral trait. Through comparing the developmental process within the twin pair and between other identical

1. From the New York State Psychiatric Institute and the Department of Psychiatry, College of Physicians and Surgeons, Columbia University, New York, N.Y.

Presented at the Annual Meeting of the American Psychosomatic Society, May 2, 1959.

Received for publication September 15, 1959.

twins presenting similar differences in behavior it is believed that some weighting may be given to the significance of various continuing and incidental postnatal experiences (transactions) that appear related to the occurrence of particular traits. Thus the design of the study offers the opportunity of examining the significance of life experiences with more certainty, as the genetic factor is held constant in the identical twin pair. Also it follows from the design of this clinical study that the significance of particular life experiences may be determined, and perhaps be given a quantitative weighting as well, by studying their occurrence in identical twins with concordance for the trait. Furthermore, this design allows a new means for verifying or modifying the hypotheses of other retrospective examinations of the developmental process.

While the potential value of such an approach is evident, its complexity must not be overlooked. It may be assumed generally that the genic pattern of identical twins is likewise identical. However, the pathway from this postulated molecular structure to the manifestation in later life of a behavioral trait is a tortuous one. Modern genetic theories do not preclude changes in gene action due to minor shifts in the balance of forces in the total chromosomal or nuclear structure, which thereafter perpetuate themselves via divergent biochemical pathways, while interactional patterns during embryonic life leading to gross phenotypic differences can only broadly be subsumed under the heading of "expressivity." Intensive study of dissimilar pairs is bound to throw light on important developmental phenomena.

Etiology of Homosexuality

Theories of the etiology of homosexuality range from those that consider the homosexual as a genetic intersex with female chromosome structure to those that consider him as a product of social or interfamilial pressure. The former theories, akin to Goldschmidt's biological findings in lower organisms (*45*), were based on the supposed preponderance of males among the siblings of homosexuals (*90*) and either infertility or the production of only females in their offspring. These findings were supposed to follow from the possession of two X chromosomes in the genetic structure of the individual, and are now subject to more definitive study since the development of facile methods of determining chromosomal sex (*113*). Although there is evidence that as many as one male in 400 has two X chromosomes (*113A*), a number of studies thus far have failed to establish this female sex chromatin pattern in male homosexuals (*119,125*). This is not surprising, since various forms of hermaphroditism or eunuchoidism have never been shown to be connected with homosexual wishes or behavior *(109,110)*.

Twin and family studies of homosexuality have suggested that genetic mechanisms of some kind may play a part in the process of psychosexual maturation leading to overt homosexual behavior. The largest series of twins was reported by Kallmann, who compared 40 monozygotic and 45 dizygotic male twin pairs *(75)*. Although procedural difficulties prevented extension of this study, the homosexuality rate among dizygotic co-twins of homosexual males did not appear to differ significantly from that among brothers. In either category, about 60 per cent revealed no evidence of overt adult homosexual experience, a figure similar to Kinsey's rate for the whole male population. In the monozygotic pairs, on the other hand, all were fully concordant as to the regular and overt practice of homosexuality, although no mutuality was ever reported. In his original study, Kallmann viewed homosexual behavior in the adult male as an "alternative minus variant" in the integrative process of psychosexual maturation rather than as a simple and codifiable entity. Postulating that the attainment of a maturational balance may be disarranged at different developmental stages and by a variety of disturbing mechanisms, he stated:

> . . . the general conclusion that habitual predominance of a homosexual behavior pattern results from disturbing experiences only in a *limited* number of persons, by no means minimizes the psychodynamic significance of these constellational factors in potentially vulnerable individuals.

In *Three Essays on the Theory of Sexuality*, Freud *(38)* expressed a similar opinion:

> The nature of inversion is explained neither by the hypothesis that is innate nor by the alternative hypothesis that it is acquired. In the former case we must ask in what respect it is innate, unless we are to accept the crude explanation that everyone is born with his sexual instinct attached to a particular sexual object. In the latter case it may be questioned whether the various accidental influences would be sufficient to explain the acquisition of inversion without the cooperation of something in the subject himself. The existence of this last factor is not to be denied.

According to psychoanalytic theories, heterosexual object choice in the male homosexual is excluded by fear of the female due to early castration anxiety or disappointment concerning the mother. The individual thus identifies with the frightening or frustrating mother and loves other men as he wished to be loved himself. Further, he may in his identification seek to be loved as she is by the father. Thus simultaneously he accomplishes a passive submission to the fearful male as a way of checking competitive hatred in the rivalry situation. Such rivalry may also occur between brothers.

These conceptual schemes provide various means to understand the motivational context in which the homosexual conflict appears. However, as Freud suggested, they do not explain why this conflict develops only in certain persons, and why only in certain persons is it overtly manifested. It is actually to this age-old problem of symptom choice, if you will, that a combined genetic and developmental study may be directed.

Differences in Twin Personality Development

Before turning to the plan of twin investigation and to the case material, it is important to bear in mind that psychoanalytic observation of twins in the past has found that certain phases of personality development differ from those found among children brought up in ordinary sibship families or as only children *(19)*. These phases lead to exaggerated conflicts and tendencies toward specific adaptations. They are briefly summarized as follows:

The maternal attitude towards twins is often one of rejection and shame, followed later by preoccupation with an exploration of the similarities and differences in the twins. Twins that cannot be easily distinguished frequently induce maternal anxiety in her need to determine which child is to obtain from her an appropriate show of emotion. Since some mothers consciously indicate their inability to love until a difference is found, the search for distinguishing marks is of significance. Insistence on similarity, on the other hand, may represent an exhibitionistic and narcissistic pleasure on the part of the mother.

The paternal attitude toward twins may be either rejection of the twins as burdensome, or pride in them as evidence of the father's sexual capacities.

The twin pair may have difficulty in establishing strong self-images if they identify with each other. The constant emotional and psychological closeness may interfere with the independent development of learned functions. Also, twins usually have an intense rivalry problem to which they may adapt by attaching themselves to one or the other parent or by always adopting the same desires and sacrificing individual drives. Intense jealousy thus generates exaggerated hostile death wishes toward each other that in turn demand compensatory efforts at repression, again bringing the twins together. These problems, of course, are not inevitable, but they represent extreme forms of intrafamily adaptive mechanisms which must be understood and taken into consideration in the clinical investigation or management of families with twins. They may exist in all twins, identical or not, although they may be presumed to play a stronger and more persistent role, the more similar the twins happen to be.

Observations

In planning the study of divergent sexual behavioral patterns as they exist in identical twins, a search was made for appropriate twin pairs. A survey of a considerable number of one-egg pairs over the past 4 years yielded only two pairs with overt differentiation in behavior.[2] The first was a female pair diagnosed as schizophrenic with differences in their sexual roles, as yet unexpressed by actual sexual contact. The second was a male pair, psychoneurotic, with one exclusively and consistently overtly homosexual in his behavior, the other similarly heterosexual.

The plan was to investigate the twins, preferably by the free-association method and by family and social studies, looking for the patterns of interpersonal interaction which influenced their psychosexual development, and to study their similarities and differences through physical, biological (biochemical and tissue studies), and psychological examinations.

Twin Pair 1

The first pair of identical twins presented divergent development in their sexual role pattern not accompanied in the "homosexual" twin by intimate genital contact with a member of the same sex. Their study was important as a means of exploring the methods of later examinations. Rosalind and Roberta, as we may call them, were born unwanted: the mother, desiring more time to care for her firstborn, a son, attempted unsuccessfully to abort when she found she was pregnant again. The first born, Rosalind, has the heterosexual orientation. The second born,

---

2. Since this paper was presented, two additional twin pairs have been found with divergent sexual development.

Roberta, was given a derivative of a boy's name intentionally by the parents. The mother was able to distinguish them immediately, as Rosalind had a small birthmark on the forearm and upper lip. These marks were frequently sought for by the mother, maternal grandmother, and maternal aunt who examined and constantly touched them. Since the focus of interest rested in pointing out Rosalind's distinguishing physical feature, Roberta received much less physical handling and caressing than her sister.

The favored child developed a heterosexual orientation and was the less disturbed in her psychosis, and the child with the homosexual role was the one rejected by both parents. Before the age of five she was severely mistreated by the father, who beat her and chained her in the basement. She was unfortunate in having no person outside the family with whom to identify, and seems to have established a hostile identification with the male parent, whom she saw as dominant and threatening. Since both parents were felt to prefer boys, this identification apparently meant greater acceptance and represented a reaction formation against the feminine role of her sister. It is interesting to note that in later life her delusional system was fixed upon the need to develop a venous marking on the forearm, which would at once give her a distinguishing mark like her sister and establish her as a boy and man.

Although neither member of this pair was amenable to free-association investigation, study of the pair helped in the formulation of the factors to be considered in later work. Thus it was decided to direct particular attention to the examination of the prenatal attitudes of each parent to the birth, their fantasies in regard to the desired sex of the child, their attitude at birth (pleased, anxious, expectant), and the family significance of the names chosen. Further important parental attitudes were those relating to bodily differences in the twins as a means of distinguishing them and their later relationship to each twin. This material was sought through interviews with both parents.

From the twins, data were elicited comparing their psychopathology, as well as their attitudes to their bodies and body parts, their self-concept as the result of the family interactional pattern from which these attitudes derived, their attitudes to being a twin and to separation from the twin, and their fantasy and dream life, important experiences, and significant relationships with others.

Twin Pair 2

Soon after the first pair of twins was seen, a 29-year-old male clerical employee, who may be called Tom, presented himself for treatment with complaints of disliking his job and having difficulty in relating to people, especially women. He was taken into psychoanalytic therapy. His twin Dick, discovered to be living an active homosexual life, was asked to come in for studies, including 25 hours of free-association interview, for which he was compensated. He has maintained his disinterest in therapy and in changing his sexual orientation.

These twins were born to parents who already had a daughter. The parents desired sons. The twins could be distinguished at birth, since Dick, the later homosexual twin, had a more pronounced split in his lower lip due to a defective closure in the median labial fissure. This fact was revealed only through interviews with the parents and a search of old pictures. Dick was further singled out by the cold and inhibited mother because he was supposed to be the weaker, although it is possible she had an earlier preference for Tom. At any rate, Tom was associated in the mind of the mother with a difficult and severe labor to which she referred many physical disabilities and for which she often blamed him in later life. Named for his father, and rejected by his mother, he found warmth and support in his paternal grandmother and a young nursemaid. As he repressed his jealous rage towards his brother and his fear and hatred of his parents, he became withdrawn, felt alienated, was doubtful of himself, and suffered periodic depression.

Both twins were seduced homosexually in their early adolescence, the homosexual at age 11, the heterosexual at age 13. Later they were both caught at school in some homosexual play with other boys. Only the heterosexual twin, Tom, recalls a warning and reprimand by his father for such activities. Dick's first attempts at sexual play with a girl were reported by her to her parents, an experience which was frightening to him. While the boys' parents discouraged both of them in their contacts with girls, Tom had his first heterosexual experience in his late teens, while his brother Dick began a long series of homosexual attachments. The parents became aware of the latter activity when he was expelled from college. The mother has maintained a permissive and denying attitude in regard to his homosexuality, visiting him and his male paramour in their apartment. The other twin, Tom, after a series of affairs with older women, married during the course of his psychoanalysis. The marriage has been satisfactory over a period of a few years, although no child as yet has been conceived.

Physiological Data

In these twins, zygosity was determined by the similarity method as outlined by Smith and Penrose (*146*); based on the seven blood groups for which the twins are identical, as well as on fingerprint analysis (*117*), the probability of their being monozygotic is .9954.

Steroid analysis was carried out on 24-hour urine specimens collected on both twins under identical controlled conditions in the hospital (by Dr. Perry R. Hudson). The identity of the steroid substances was established by detailed chromatographic and spectrophotometric procedures, including infrared analysis.

Eleven steroid substances were detected in the specimens of both twins. The most abundant steroid found in both in approximately equal quantities was 11-beta-17-alpha-20-beta 21-tetrahydroxy-delta$_4$ pregnene-3. This is a normal urinary metabolite of cortisol, the major steroid known to be secreted by the human adrenol. Four 17-ketosteroids, androsterone being the most obvious, were detected in both specimens. Thus, urinary steroid patterns of these twins were qualitatively and quantitatively similar.

Chromosomal sex determinations using specimens of buccal mucosa were obtained (by Dr. Melvin Grumbach). These revealed a male chromatin pattern in both.

Psychological Test Findings

The psychological test findings[3] on Tom and Dick taken at the beginning of Tom's treatment presented interesting similarities and dissimilarities. In general, intellectual functions were similar, with each twin functioning at the bright normal level of intelligence. (Tom's I.Q., 117; Dick's I.Q., 113). While hewing to a much more conventional approach to life's problems than Dick, Tom appeared relatively less able to operate productively and creatively. In spite of the dissimilarity of their overt expression in the sexual area, underlying conflicts and unconscious motivations were strikingly similar. Marked sexual confusion was apparent in each record and would not have distinguished one twin from the other. Tom (heterosexual) demonstrated a greater need to present a heterosexual façade and gave Rorschach responses including a vagina, penis, and anus. Dick's (homosexual) record

---

3. The following tests were administered: Wechsler Adult Intelligence Scale, Rorschach, Sentence Completion, Second Body Cathexis Scale, Draw-a-Person, and Bender Gestalt tests.

included only anal-sexual responses. The distortion in body image appeared greater in Tom; his figure drawings showed greater confusion and his expressed dissatisfaction with his own body was more marked. Anxiety and feelings of depression were also greater in Tom's protocol. In terms of the over-all evaluation of the data, Dick showed evidence of less anxiety, with ego defenses more effective than those of Tom in spite of the less conventional sexual adaptation of the former.

Discussion

In its design, this study differs from previous efforts to examine the human developmental process. The genetic factor may be assumed as constant through selection of identical twin pairs with divergent psychosexual roles as subjects. It must be emphasized again that the finding of suitable subjects for such studies is most difficult. Not only are such twin pairs rare but also the design is impaired in this instance through inability to have one of the male twins motivated for psychoanalysis and to find both of the female pair able to communicate to the point of providing free-association material. Nevertheless, in the male pair, the homosexual twin did provide free-association material pertinent to elucidating his developmental experiences over a 25-hour period when offered his expenses for the time given. Material obtained through free association over brief periods and under similar circumstances has been used by others in the past to construct a definition of personality development, and such information has been found similar to that obtained under the usual circumstances of psychoanalytic practice where the patient is required to pay a fee. From the standpoint of the writers a greater defect exists in the fact that the homosexual twin was studied by the free-association method over a period of approximately one-tenth the time that the heterosexual was studied. In the case of the heterosexual twin, highly significant data, particularly in relation to experiences with important extrafamilial female figures, were obtained only after hours of free association. Nevertheless, it is believed that this pilot study has disclosed a series of parental attitudes and transactions with each twin that led to the resulting overtly variant sexual behaviors.

Psychosexual confusion coupled with body image distortion were found in both twins in psychological testing, but were greater in degree in the heterosexual twin. There existed in each of these brothers an increased body preoccupation. More intense in the heterosexual twin, it showed itself in extreme self-devaluation, sexual confusion, and poor self-identity. The homosexual brother also showed some self-derogation when interviewed, but there had been less parental devaluation and a better sense of self-identity existed from early years. Aided by these factors, but more fearfully involved with his mother, he had been able to transfer his concern from his own body to another person of the same sex and achieve some kind of love relationship in a homosexual attachment.

The mother blamed the last-born heterosexual for her difficult labor and subsequent invalidism, and by distinguishing the two through slight physical differences, admittedly bestowed preferential physical contact on the other. Considering his brother to be his mother's favorite, the heterosexual twin was estranged from his mother. It became clear in his analysis that his estrangement was basically self-imposed and determined by guilt relating to his repressed rage towards his mother and brother. With this separation from the mother he obtained his satisfactions from a kind and accepting grandmother, a warm and feminine nursemaid, and some degree of guidance from an otherwise passive father. From them he turned in early adulthood to a series of immature and compulsive heterosexual attachments, with concomitant submergence of his aggressivity, which have been interpreted as a reaction formation against his own homosexual fears.

The homosexual twin, on the other hand, was held closely to the mother who preferred him, overprotected him as being physically less able than his brother, derogated his father to him, frustrated his attempts to contact girls, and acted permissively towards his homosexual life — a family pattern which one of us has defined earlier as leading to overt homosexual activity (*84*). His homosexual pattern also represents a submissive adaptation to an originally aggressive brother.

The paternal relationship was significant in establishing a heterosexual role for the maternally rejected twin by providing him a focus for masculine identification and also through establishing a masculine ideal through nonpermissiveness regarding homosexual behavior.

It may be noted that biologically the socially appropriate sexual behavior in these twins appears unrelated to the quantity or degree of the psychopathology. Moreover, homosexual seduction in itself did not determine overt homosexual behavior in adulthood, since both twins were seduced between the ages of 11 and 13.

Thus, this study sought for differences in the developmental processes of these one-egg twins which might help to explain the alternate modes of preferred sexual gratification eventually evolved. The parents of these twins had wanted a boy and upon their birth sought for distinguishing body features. The mother created an especially close bond between herself and the first born twin who had the distinguishing facial feature, was supposed to be the weaker, and had not injured her during pregnancy. Body ego development, poor for both, was less pathological for this twin. Nevertheless, fearful and frustrated in his close maternal relationship, he apparently formed a hostile identification with her which contributed to his homosexual pattern. The less-favored twin, his greater strength only a source of guilt to him, withdrew from the mother and did form an identification with the father. Because of the father's own weakness, this identification did not provide a significant ideal image, yet revealed itself in analysis to have been a potential source of ego strength. Most significant for his future object relationships were female figures other than his parents – namely his grandmother and the nursemaid. As he grew, he developed reaction formations against both aggressivity and the homosexual adaptation which his brother assumed. Homosexual dreams in this twin occurred only once during his analysis, and then as a reaction to a currently disturbing conception of heterosexuality as murderous aggression towards the woman. As can be seen, the factors which operated in the differentiation of sexual roles in the female twins were similar to those reported in this male pair, except that in the instance of the homosexual girl twin there was an absence of interpersonal relations outside the family.

Summary

Two sets of homosexual twins, one male and the other female, have been studied in whom the development of the overt psychosexual role was divergent in the sense that one of each pair was heterosexual while the other was homosexual. In the male pair the roles were overtly determined to the extent of genital satisfaction; in the adolescent female pair the roles were determined but without as yet overt sexual intimacies.

The determining life experiences for the differentiation of the sexual role were found in the prenatal fantasies of the parents of one pair for a child different from that of the twins at birth; and a slight but definite anatomical differentiation in the twins which determined for the mother a special attachment for one or the other child. There resulted early differentiation of the body ego for each of the individuals and later in life enhancement of the sexual role through the existence or deprivation of significant extrafamilial relations. Of significance also was the parental attitude toward the role of the individual child disclosed through the naming of the child.

Biologically appropriate sexual behavior was unrelated to the type or degree of psychopathology.

Homosexual seduction in itself was not found to determine homosexual behavior nor deter heterosexual behavior.

Neurological and various biochemical examinations failed to reveal differences between these identical twin pairs divergent for homosexuality and heterosexuality.

Discussion

Franz J. Kallmann

Contrary to what my reputation may lead one to expect, my real goal is to help in promoting pluridimensional concepts of etiology which would fully reconcile current psychodynamic and psychogenetic theories of disordered behavior, in sex maturation patterns as well as in other areas of personality integration. I am delighted, therefore, to have been invited to discuss this interesting report by my colleagues at the New York State Psychiatric Institute. Having had no hand in this well-presented study, I am free to underscore its good timing and unquestionable significance.

It is gratifying, although by no means unexpected, that the search for a one-egg pair of nonschizophrenic males, found at age 30 to be dissimilar as to overt homosexuality, has at long last been successful. Even if this were not a single pair, it would be immaterial whether such twins were classified as partly concordant for homosexual behavior or as largely discordant. Certainly the twin who is now heterosexual falls below Group 3 on Kinsey's rating scale, which was used in our earlier study of twin sibships (*75*).

Methodologically, it is more important that, in a series of one-egg twins, a 100 per cent concordance rate is regarded as a mere statistical artifact even in a highly specific sequence of faulty biosynthetic steps triggered by a major mutant gene. Indeed, the assumption of such a fixed relationship between primary gene effect and its behavioral endpoint would put us back in that unhappy stage when a genetic hypothesis was a wastebasket abstraction about which one knew little and could do even less (*76*). Fortunately, recent advances in psychogenetics have been so remarkable that numerous subbasement structures of genically disarranged behavior patterns no longer deserve the label *terra incognita* (*51*).

As to the genetic aspects of male homosexuality, no biologist would assume that "the tendency to substitute reproductively nonsignificant sexual goals for a mate of the opposite sex" (*72*) is reducible to a homogeneous maturational deficiency produced by a single genetic factor. Obviously, the potentials for a mature form of sexual behavior depend on the balanced effect of many genes, and the concept of a coadapted polygenic system implies that different genetic mechanisms may produce correlated responses. Known to have pleiotropic effects, polygenes can act both as modifiers of traits for which no major gene differences are demonstrable (*94*).

To do justice to both psychoanalytic and genetic data on homosexuality, it has been suggested that the most probable mode of operation of its gene-specific components with a pleiotropic effect may be "on the rates of development of neuropsychological mechanisms involved in identification processes and other aspects of object relation in infancy" (*72*). At the present stage of information it is quite possible that this somewhat overgeneralized hypothesis is the simplest explanation of the observations made in twin studies.

Even if this hypothesis should ultimately have to be modified as additional facts are provided by new research methods, I am confident that the histories of the twins studied so painstakingly by Dr. Rainer and his co-workers will prove of lasting value.   We know that many important discoveries have come from investigations undertaken to explore some hypothesis that later called for refinement (*36*).

A Pair of Male
Monozygotic Twins
Discordant for Homosexuality

Gordon K. Klintworth,[1] M.B., B. Ch.

Homosexuality has puzzled man since time immemorial, and as a result of its being insufficiently understood numerous fanciful etiological theories have emerged, among which cultural, sociological or psychological factors have been variously felt to be of primary importance. On the other hand, many have felt that it is due to a multiplicity of causes (*162*). Twin studies are often the most satisfactory method of determining the role of genetic factors in the causation of pathological disorders. By means of this approach, convincing evidence in support of an hereditary factor being the most important in the etiology of homosexuality has been put forward. The twin studies of Kallmann (*77, 75*) are the most comprehensive to date. Kallmann studied 85 homosexuals who had twin brothers. Of 45 dizygotic male twin pairs psychosexual information was available in 26. The homosexuality rate among these dizygotic co-twins did not differ significantly from that among their brothers. In the case of the monozygotic twins, there were three co-twins who could not be classified

1. Department of Pathology, Duke University Medical Center, Durham, North Carolina. (From the Departments of Anatomy and Psychological Medicine, University of the Witwatersrand, Johannesburg, Republic of South Africa.) The author wishes to thank Professors L. A. Hurst and P. V. Tobias for encouragement and assistance in this study; Dr. F. J. Kallmann for his report on the fingerprints; Professor C. J. Dreyer and Dr. J. F. van Reenan for taking and reporting the dental impressions; Dr. J. Kaufmann for the histological examinations; Dr. J. de Boer for the blood groups; Mrs. L. C. M. Lambert, Mr. R. P. Gluckman and Dr. A. Lazarus for the projective psychological tests; the photographic unit of the Department of Medicine of the University of the Witwatersrand, Johannesburg, for the photography.

psychosexually. He found the remaining 37 one-egg twins to be fully concordant as to the overt practice of homosexuality. Kallmann stated that all of the concordant twin partners denied any history of mutuality in overt sex relations. He also pointed out that many of them claimed to have developed their often very similar sexual patterns independently and far apart from each other. These studies strongly supported the hypothesis that homosexuality was genetically determined and was independent of environmental influences.

Recently, a male passive homosexual (Figures 1-3)[2] was admitted to the Department of Psychological Medicine at the Johannesburg General Hospital. He mentioned that he had a twin brother (Figures 4-6) of similar appearance whom he thought was heterosexual. As this case apparently differed from those of Kallmann, it was felt that the twin pair should be fully investigated in order to determine firstly the zygosity of the twins and secondly whether they were concordant or not.

Materials and Methods

A detailed history was obtained from both twins. In addition, both had a complete physical examination. When the heterosexual twin was approached he first treated the matter with contempt, but after the investigator persisted, he agreed to cooperate in the investigation.

Photographs of the twins during infancy were obtained from the parents (Figures 7-9). Full blood grouping of both twins as well as of their parents was determined. The saliva of the twins was tested for ABO secretor activity. Fingerprints and dental impressions were taken. The twins were tested independently for color blindness, using Ishihara charts, and their taste threshold to phenylthiocarbamide was determined, using the method of Harris and Kalmus (*58*). The sex chromatin was ascertained from skin biopsies of both twins. A full depth 2 cm. square of skin was grafted from the forearm of each twin to that of the other (Figures 10-11). The grafts were observed at regular intervals and after eight weeks a transverse biopsy was taken across the whole graft including normal skin on both sides. This was histologically examined. Twenty-four-hour specimens of urine from the homosexual twin were tested for follicle stimulating hormone, 17-ketosteroids and 17-hydroxycorticosteroids. Projective psychological tests were

---

2. The photographs of the twins are not reprinted here. They show strikingly similar, freckled young men differing mildly in hairstyle (the homosexual's hair style is closer to a pompadour, while the heterosexual's is a kind of crew cut), the twins as infants, and the twins' forearms before and after the skin transplant.

performed on both twins. After the Thematic Apperception Test had been carried out on the heterosexual twin the record was submitted to three independent psychologists for interpretation. Initially, they were given no information about this study in order that their opinions would be as unbiased as possible. After their initial report they were asked whether there was any evidence of homosexuality.

Case Report

John, a 20-year-old white male, was admitted to the Johannesburg General Hospital in December, 1959, having attempted suicide by cutting both his wrists and taking an overdose of aspirin and Noludar. He had been depressed following a recent passive homosexual experience. During his first job (as a bank clerk) at the age of 16, he first began to feel sexually attracted towards men. He would picture himself as a girl and a certain man as his boy friend. He stated, "I would see a man and wish I could go out with him. I would fall in love with about one in every twenty men I saw." He felt self-conscious about this "peculiar sexual attraction" but did not discuss it with anyone. He said, "The males to whom I am attracted are quite serious and take an active part in the same kind of sport as me. They are good-looking and well spoken. I can't describe them any better." When he first noticed this attraction to individuals of his own sex he was not worried, as he did not consider it abnormal and had always considered himself to be feminine in his mannerisms. He did not tell anyone about his feelings as he thought that they would laugh at him. It was only when he was 17 years old that he heard about homosexuality. At that age he developed a platonic friendship with a colleague four years his senior. He does not think that this friend realized that he was a homosexual. After going out together for two years his friend changed his job and was transferred many miles away. This resulted in the patient becoming severely depressed. "I was most upset for about a week. This was followed by a blank in my mind which must have lasted another week. I was found in a hotel many miles from home. I don't know how I got there. This is the only time in my life that I have had such a breakdown. I remained upset for a couple of weeks after the blackout and did not want to see anybody. I was visited by my family doctor who referred me to a psychiatrist, with whom I discussed my problems. I only saw the psychiatrist once as I was afraid to talk about my homosexuality." He had no further close friendships with the male sex. In November 1959, while having a meal in a cafe, he was approached by a man six years his senior. This man said that he had heard that the patient was a homosexual and that he would like to have sexual relations with him. They went to the man's flat where the patient had his first homosexual experience. He was the passive partner and enjoyed it at the time, but afterwards became depressed and attempted suicide. It was this suicide attempt that resulted in his admission to the Johannesburg Hospital.

Differences and Similarities
between the Twins

Early development: The twins were born in 1939. The firstborn, John, weighed five and one-quarter pounds at birth. Shortly afterwards his twin brother was delivered, having a birth weight of five and three-quarter pounds. Ever since birth George has been slightly heavier than John. The twins were delivered at home by a district midwife. Nothing is known about the placenta and membranes. It was about four days after their birth that it was noted that both had a "tongue tie." The midwife treated this herself with a pair of scissors. Both were breast-fed for one month and then bottle-fed for nine months. Solids were commenced at the age of six months. Their mother does not recall any differences in their feeding habits. John was "a very good child and not naughty like other children," whereas his twin was "like most boys." As far as their mother can recall, their teeth erupted at the same age. George commenced walking and talking a month before John. During their childhood it was only the homosexual twin who had neurotic symptoms. He sucked his thumb at the age of eight to nine years. He could not stand being alone in a room "because I thought that there was something in the room which I could not see." Between the ages of ten and twelve he had periodic bouts of somnambulism.

Family history and interpersonal relationships: The father was a healthy 48-year-old shop assistant. He did not appear to favor any particular member of the family. Although none of children got on well with him, it was perhaps John who was the most rejected by him. Both twins maintained in interview that they had had difficulty in reaching a satisfactory rapport with their father. The mother was four years younger than their father. She had chronic rheumatic carditis with mitral stenosis and was under the constant supervision of a physician. In addition, she was an inadequate personality prone to depressive episodes and latterly addicted to Noludar. She was well known to the writer and was in fact admitted to the Johannesburg Hospital soon after the patient because of a suicidal attempt. This she did, so she said, "because his admission to hospital came as a severe shock to me." Although she stated that she was not aware that he was a homosexual she had been suspicious that there "was something wrong with his sex." Both twins had been closely attracted to her and preferred her to their father. George was of the opinion that his twin was his mother's favorite "because he can't stand on his own." The parents had been divorced for the past two years but still regularly visited each other. Besides the twins, there were two other siblings, an elder brother, aged 23, and a young sister of 13. The twins had never been close friends and after going to high school they drifted apart completely due to different interests.

Hobbies and interests: As a child the patient always preferred to play with girls' toys. This interest was observed prior to the age of four. George, on the other hand, played with the usual toys that interest a boy; *e.g.*, cars, trains and soldiers. While at school John developed an interest in singing and recitation and regularly took part in the *Eisteddfod* where he received numerous awards. His twin was not interested in such matters. During high school George was most interested in building and flying model aeroplanes. Since leaving school he has been attentive to films, but does not have any real preferences. George is fond of jazz and plays snooker and darts approximately twice a week. John prefers classical music, does pewter work as a hobby and is interested in sewing and cooking. This does not interest his twin. George is very fond of riding a motor bike, whereas his twin dislikes it.

Sports: When the boys were at primary school they both played tennis and soccer. At high school George continued to play tennis but also took up rugby and cricket. He eventually became captain of the school first cricket and tennis teams. He played in the third rugby team. Both twins were strong tennis players and competition between them was keen. After a tough battle it was usually George who took the match. John still plays tennis but George lost interest in it when he started work and prefers to drink and play darts with his friends. While at high school John went in for physical training and athletics in addition to tennis. George, although taking part in the former, did not have much interest in them.

Friends: Until they went to high school the twins had many friends in common. It was John, however, who played almost entirely with girls between the ages of four and 12. At twelve, both went to boarding school where they mixed with boys and girls. John had no real interest in either sex and although he got on well with many of his schoolmates he had only two close boy friends. George, on the other hand, was much more popular and had many friends, including a few girls.

Sexual education and behavior: It was from their classmates that they both learned about sex when they were about ten. The information seemingly did not come as a surprise and did not worry them. At about this age their elder brother and cousin masturbated in front of them. From then onwards they began to masturbate. This apparently did not cause any feelings of guilt, as they both considered it as normal behavior. Although George denies fantasies when masturbating, John stated that from the age of 16 he always pictured himself as a girl having sexual intercourse with a man. He still has such mental images as he masturbates. George started to go out with girls when he was 13 and is sexually attracted to girls. He has had about 20 girl friends and first had sexual intercourse three years ago. For the past two years, he has been intimate almost every week with one of three girl friends. The homosexual twin, on the other hand, has taken out only two or three girls and has kissed them. This resulted in no "sexual feeling." He has had no other heterosexual experiences and has never had a desire to have sexual intercourse with a member of the opposite sex. From the age of six, John wanted to be a girl and had the desire to dress in girls' clothing. At that age he did in fact dress up in woman's clothing on about three occasions. He liked it immensely and would have done it more often but felt that "it should not be done." He stated, nevertheless, that this desire to dress in the clothing of the opposite sex has not been very strong.   However, the longing to change his sex has been pronounced and he has lived with the hope that he could have an operation which would allow him to become a female. He remembers once reading about such an operation in a newspaper. John has had no urge to have children. The homosexual inclinations of the patient are described above. His co-twin has emphatically denied any homosexual thoughts or experiences at any stage of his life. This has been in spite of strong reassurance that all information supplied by him would be treated with the strictest of confidence. The importance of accuracy in his history was also explained to him.

Education: They started school at the same primary school when they were six years old. Both passed Standard Five at the age of 12. It is reported that they got on well with the teachers and school children. At school the teachers always considered the twins "as one." While at primary school George usually came first or second in the class and consistently did better than John, who most often came second or third. They were both very good at history, arithmetic and languages. Between the ages of 12 and 16 they went to a coeducational high school as boarders.   There they were most successful in bookkeeping and commerce and had difficulty with mathematics.   While at high school they ranked about tenth in class. It was at this period, however, that John began to get higher marks than George.   Throughout their schooling they always remained in the same class. Both were fond of all aspects of their education and were keen on matriculating, but on their father's recommendation they left school at the age of 16 after passing their Junior Certificate (Standard Eight).

Occupations: After leaving school the twins entered different occupations. George became an apprentice fitter and turner, while John started work as a bank clerk, as he was not interested in a trade. After about two and a half years, John was offered a post on the clerical staff of the same firm as his twin. In view of better prospects he accepted this job and has remained there ever since.

In was in the latter job that the homosexual twin began to have difficulty with the male tradesmen. "They whistled at me like a person whistles at a girl. They also made silly remarks such as 'We would like to take you out.' They appeared to be aware of my homosexuality." He got on well with the clerical staff who were nearly all women. The heterosexual twin had a satisfactory interpersonal relationship with all his co-workers.

Residence: The twins lived at home with parents and siblings until the age of 12. At that time their parents sold the house and the boys were sent to boarding school, where they remained until they left school at the age of 16. Both then continued to live at home until their parents' divorce in 1957. Subsequently they boarded with separate friends.

Antisocial behavior: George once had his name taken by the police at the age of 19 "because of disturbing the peace by being too noisy on the way home from a party where I had too much to drink." This was the only time that he had been in trouble with the police.

Past illnesses: Except for the usual childhood diseases medical histories were essentially negative. At the age of six both had tonsillectomies. They had chickenpox together when they were seven; a short while later both of them developed measles.

Habits:

> *Alcohol:* George drinks an occasional beer during the week, but at the weekend he reports consuming up to three-fourths of a bottle of brandy. John never drinks.
>
> *Cigarettes:* Both twins smoke twenty to thirty cigarettes per day.
>
> *Drugs:* When he was 18 years old George smoked "dagga" (Cannabis sativa) on one occasion. He disliked it and had not tried it since then. His twin has never taken it or any other drugs.

Physical examination: The twins resembled each other in appearance. The homosexual, although of slightly lighter complexion than his co-twin, was of a similar body build. They had light ginger hair with identical scalp hair. Their ear patterns were similar and both had very little fissuring of the tongue. A Grade 3 mandibular prognathism was present in both twins. Their eyes were greenish grey in color, and the left was dominant in both the homosexual and his co-twin. Minimal hair was present on the chest of both twins and their bodies were both covered with prominent ephelides which were similarly distributed. They were both right-handed and had identical palmar creases. A mild degree of clinodactyly was noted in the little fingers of both members of the pair. Hair was present on the middle phalanx of only the fourth and fifth fingers of both hands in both individuals. The feet were of similar size, had identical plantar creases and the hallux was the largest toe. The remaining toes were progressively smaller. The homosexual twin was left-footed and the heterosexual right-footed.

Results of Investigations

Blood-groups: The twin pair had identical blood groups. They both were A_1, Rh negative (heterozygous), M Ns, P, Kell negative, Duffy negative, Le^a negative and C_w negative. The father had the same blood groups and the mother differed only in being N N_s and not M Ns.

ABO secretor activity in the twins: This was present in both twins.

Fingerprints: These were submitted to Dr. F. Kallmann who reported: "On the basis of a detailed statistical analysis of the fingerprints of the twins, it is impossible to classify this pair as either monozygotic or dizygotic, as the ridge counts and pattern counts fall within the monozygotic-dizygotic overlap group."

Dental impressions: Professor C. J. Dreyer, of the University of the Witwatersrand Dental Research Unit, compared the dental impressions of the twins. He observed that there was contraction of the maxillary arch associated with a high vault of the palate, lingual inclination of the mandibular buccal segments and an anterior open bite in the homosexual twin. These abnormalities are all consistent with an abnormal swallowing habit.

Tests of color-blindness: The twin pair both displayed the classical features of the completely green-blind variety of red-green color-blindness.

Taste threshold to phenylthiocarbamide: Both twins tasted phenylthiocarbamide in low dilutions. The homosexual twin tasted it in a dilution of 5.08 mgm/ml and his co-twin in a dilution of 2.54 mgm/ml.

Sex chromatin: Sections from skin biopsies of both twins were cut at different levels and stained with three different stains. They showed the presence of sex chromatin in less than 5 per cent of the nuclei of the epidermis, sweat glands, and muscle in both twins. Their nuclear sex is therefore that of the normal male.

Skin graft: The 2 cm. square which was grafted from the heterosexual twin to the homosexual took completely (Figure 12). The heterosexual twin removed his dressing during the first week and scratched it because of itching. Nevertheless, the graft took extensively in the periphery. Histological examination of the graft after eight weeks failed to reveal any evidence of an inflammatory reaction. The junction of the graft with the normal skin could barely be detected.

Hormonal examination of urine from the homosexual twin: Twenty-four-hour specimens of urine were found to contain 13.4 mgm of 17-ketosteroids (estimated as dehydroisoandrosterone); six to twelve mouse units of follicle stimulating hormone; 5.9 mgm of 17-hydroxycorticosteroids (P. S. C.).

Projective psychological tests: These were carried out by a psychoanalytically oriented psychologist, who concluded that John's homosexuality was due to the following:

1) A passive-dependent attitude towards the mother; her inability to satisfy such demands, arousing ambivalence in the patient.

2) The possible explanation for such a strong dependence on the mother was the patient's fear of an aggressive father.

3) In order to adapt to a disciplinarian and aggressive father, the patient denied his Oedipal wishes and developed toward the father a passive, masochistic attitude, so attempting to accept symbolic castration.

4) The aggressive and violent father was not an object with which the patient could easily identify; he therefore tends to identify with the mother and lacks an appropriate ego ideal.

The Thematic Apperception Test, which was administered to the heterosexual twin, revealed an ambivalent personality whose tendency to dream (rather than to act) set up a syndrome which could easily be portrayed in terms of contrasts and apparent paradoxes. His reactions varied between clear and definite responses to certain life stimuli, and an opposite and overwhelming response of confusion and internal chaos. He was seen as ambitious but without goals; his hostility had intrapunitive elements. His general anxiety seemed to be related to his inability to express his hostility in an adequate way. Yet, this is a man who cannot understand basic feelings other than in terms of aggression.

Even more distressing for him is the fact that he is terrified of his own aggression and has difficulty in suppressing it because he lives in a threatening world. He seems to function best on a level of withdrawal, especially when external pressures demand a definite course of action. Apart from occasional and immature outbursts of emotion, he appears capable only of having shallow emotionality in his interpersonal relationships. There was nothing in the record to suggest homosexuality. It is, however, doubted by some as to whether projective tests *per se* can ever reveal anything more than broad personality outline. Special psychological tests, such as those of Terman and Miles (*153*) have been developed to differentiate one sex from another; these tests unfortunately were not available during the present study.

Discussion

In the diagnosis of twin zygosity much attention has been paid in the past to the examination of the fetal membranes, as it was generally believed that one-egg twins would have a single placenta and chorion with two amniotic sacs; two-egg twins were thought to be present when two placentæ, chorionic sacs and amniotic membranes were present. It is now well known that this method is fallacious, as monozygotic twins may have two placentæ, choria and amniotic membranes. The similarity method of classifying twins is widely used today. The more alike a twin pair is in variable physical features, the more probable are they to be identical. The utilization of factors that are largely the result of heredity are most important. Among the latter are the blood groups, fingerprints, and ability to taste phenylthiocarbamide. If twins differ in their blood groups they cannot be MZ in type but if they are similar they may or may not be identical. Methods of establishing the probability of dizygotic and monozygotic twins have been outlined by Race and Sanger (*126*) and Smith and Penrose (*146*). The twin pair presented above was unfortunately not ideally suited to the same type of statistical analysis, as the parents had almost identical blood groups. Except for the homosexuality, and for differing maxillary arches that are consistent with an acquired abnormal swallowing pattern, the twins were similar in all respects. In order to establish the twin type with more certainty, skin grafting was performed.

It is well known that the grafting of skin from one individual to another rarely survives whereas autografts invariably take. Medawar and his co-workers (*106*) have shown that the transplantation of skin from one individual to another may appear to take initially but later to be rejected after the development of an antigen-antibody reaction. The rejection results from the differing genetic constitution of the tissues (*107*). Another exceptional instance where homografts in non-identical twins may be exchanged with impunity is when the recipient suffers from agammaglobulinemia, as an antibody response will be lacking (*31*). In the present twin study the latter condition has been excluded and, while the former situation is theoretically possible, it is believed to be extremely improbable.

It would appear, therefore, that the twin pair under discussion is, with a minimum possibility of error, monozygotic.

There are very few reports of monozygotic twins discordant for homosexuality. Furthermore, in the majority of such cases the diagnosis of one-egg twins can be accepted only with reservation.

The earliest published report on possible identical male twins who were discordant for homosexuality is that of Lange (*93*). Among his study of criminal twins were the 24-year-old brothers, Otto and Erich Hiersekorn. Otto, the homosexual, had been imprisoned as a result of his sexual activities. He had occasional intercourse with females, but without particularly caring for it. Erich, on the other hand, was purely heterosexual and emphatically denied any attraction to his own sex. It disgusted him to think of such a thing and he was unable to imagine how anyone could have anything to do with someone of the same sex. At school the twins were so similar in appearance that their teacher requested that they should wear suits of different colors in order that he could distinguish them one from the other. When Lange saw the twins he felt that it was easy to tell them apart. The homosexual had gynecomastia and other feminine characteristics which formed a strong contrast to the masculine conformation of his co-twin. The author was of the opinion that the brothers were monozygotic because of their resemblances in complexions and appearance. With the exception of one index finger, they had similar fingerprint patterns. The twins had apparently suffered from birth trauma, for the homosexual twin had a "flaccid right cheek and a facial tic." According to Lange, "an expert cannot help feeling convinced that there is some connection between this brain lesion and his sexual abnormality."

Another early twin study on homosexuality is that of Sanders (*134*), who reported his findings on eight twin pairs, seven of which were monozygotic and one dizygotic. With the exception of one female monozygotic pair that was concordant, the rest were males. Five of his male monozygotic pairs were concordant and one was discordant; of the latter pair (O and P), the homosexual (O) suffered from epilepsy between the ages of four and 14. After he turned 14, he became overtly homosexual but tried to abstain from it without success. This resulted in a severe psychological disturbance. His co-twin was heterosexual. The parents of this twin pair were first cousins. Sanders considered that the homosexuality might have been related to the presence of underlying brain disease which had manifested itself with epilepsy. He, however, drew attention to the fact that Hirschfeld (*64*), in an investigation of 40,000 epileptics, was unable to find any homosexuals among them. The dizygotic male twin pair of Sanders was discordant for homosexuality.

Rainer *et al.* (*128*) reported a study on two sets of identical twins, one male and the other female, in which one of each pair was heterosexual while the other was homosexual. They believed that "the determining life experiences for the differentiation of the sexual role were found in the prenatal fantasies of the parents of one pair for a child different in sex from that of the twins at birth; and a slight but definite anatomical differentiation in the twins which determined for the mother a special attachment for one or the other child. There resulted early differentiation of the body ego for each of the individuals and later in life enhancement of the sexual role through the existence or deprivation of significant extrafamilial relations. Of significance also was the parental attitude toward the role of the individual child disclosed through the naming of the child."

West (*21*) mentioned that he had come across a pair of seemingly identical twins, one a practicing homosexual and the other definitely not, but owing to the usual difficulties the case could not be scientifically investigated.

Kallmann (*78*) mentioned a 30-year-old pair of one-egg twins which were discordant as to both hebephrenic schizophrenia with alcoholism and exclusively homosexual behavior that had been present since adolescence. Slater (*145*) stated that the Medical Research Council at the Maudsley Hospital had investigated a monozygotic twin pair similar to Kallmann's in which the partner who had a schizophrenic illness with a fair remission was a confirmed homosexual, while his twin was not. On follow-up, the second twin was found to have become schizophrenic and had the delusion that he might be changing his sex, but no homosexual behavior had been reported. Slater has also come across other homosexual twins which were mostly alleged to be discordant but had been difficult to investigate.

The fact that discordance for homosexuality in monozygotic twins exists does not in any way invalidate the concept that overt homosexuality is a gene-controlled variant in the integrative process of psychosexual maturation. Genetic studies in many well established hereditary diseases have conclusively shown that although a mutant gene may be present it does not always produce a recognizable effect.

The occurrence of incomplete penetrance can be adequately explained by the fact that other genes and environmental factors modify the expression of the gene under consideration. Furthermore, although monozygotic twins possess similar complements of chromosomes and genes, they may receive differing quantities of cytoplasmic inclusion from the zygote. For years it has been questionable whether genetic determiners exist in the cytoplasm, but recently evidence of cytoplasmic inheritance has been produced from observations on lower forms of life (*108,116,147,159*). Although this has never been demonstrated in man it is possible that such cytoplasmic factors could affect the expressivity of genes and thus help to explain the discordance of inherited conditions that occurs in monozygotic twins.

It is generally assumed that the same complement of genes is present in both members of a one-egg-twin pair. Darlington (*26*), however, has pointed out that this is not always strictly true, as various examples are known where the monozygotic twin pair must differ in genetic structure. Slight differences in the genotype of one-egg-twins may occur through vagaries of the chiasma and crossover mechanisms. In addition, differences may be due to the reaction between the genotype and an asymmetrical cytoplasm. A possible difference in the genetic endowment of MZ twins may account for the discordance of homosexuality in certain one-egg-twins.

In psychoanalytic theories male homosexuality can be explained in a number of ways. It has been claimed that the homosexual rejects a heterosexual object choice, because of disappointment concerning the mother, or through fear of the female resulting from an early castration complex. On the other hand, an exaggerated emotional attachment to the mother is claimed to cause male homosexuality by rendering a normal heterosexual adjustment difficult or impossible due to an unconsciously conceived incestuous act. A strong identification with the mother is also said to cause a love for other men. Such explanations can be applied to most male homosexuals. An identification and over-dependence upon the mother was believed by some to be the cause of the homosexuality in the above case. But was this dependence not, in fact, due to the psychological disturbances resulting from the expression of his genotype?

The presence of red-green color-blindness in this twin pair is of interest since it is a sex-linked characteristic. This finding has not been reported in previous homosexual studies and may be coincidental.

However, since color-blindness in this twin pair is associated with an abnormality in psychosexuality, it may suggest linkage with genetic factors that control male homosexuality. Further studies in this field are therefore indicated.

Summary

A 20-year-old monozygotic twin pair discordant for male homosexuality is presented. The literature on male one-egg-twins that are alleged to be discordant for male homosexuality is reviewed. The absence of complete concordance for male homosexuality in monozygotic twins can be adequately explained in terms of well accepted genetic concepts. The homosexuality in one twin can also be construed by psychoanalytic theories.

Homosexuality in Twins:
A Family Study and a
Registry Study

L. L. Heston, M.D., Iowa City, and James Shields, B.A., London[1]

In this paper, we will report briefly on a series of male twins where at least one of each pair was homosexual. One object is to report the number of concordant and discordant, monozygotic (MZ) and dizygotic (DZ) pairs observed. A second object is to examine the frequency of homosexuality in twins per se. One of the twin pairs was from a family deserving special attention. Among 14 siblings, there were three sets of male MZ twins. Two of these three sets of twins were concordant for homosexuality; in the remaining pair both twins were heterosexual. The results of our study of this family will be presented in detail.

The use of twin studies as a means of disentangling some of the interaction of nature and nurture is sufficiently well known for it to be unnecessary to give any elaborate explanation here (*33,170*). Briefly, differences in MZ pairs provide evidence as to environmental effects.

1. Submitted for publication July 5, 1967.

From the Department of Psychiatry, State University of Iowa Medical School, Iowa City (Dr. Heston), and the Medical Research Council, Psychiatric Genetics Research Unit, Maudsley Hospital, London (Mr. Shields).

Reprint requests to 500 Newton Rd., Iowa City, Iowa 52240 (Dr. Heston).

Dr. Heston is a former Guest Worker, Psychiatric Genetics Research Unit, supported by Special Fellowship 1-F3-MH-28, 474-01 (MTLH) National Institute of Mental Health. Dr. Ruth Sanger, MRC Blood Group Research Unit, Lister Institute, London, performed the blood grouping and Dr. Elizabeth B. Robson, MCR Human Biochemical Genetics Research Unit, the Galton Laboratory, London, did the starch gel electrophoresis. Dr. F. Kräupl Taylor called our attention to the family studied. Dr. J. Kahn, Psychiatric Genetics Research Unit, prepared and read the karyotype.

The comparison of resemblance in MZ pairs, who are genetically identical, with that in DZ or genetically dissimilar pairs can provide evidence as to the likely importance of heredity.

Previous Twin Studies of Homosexuality

We will begin with a short though comprehensive survey of the findings as regards male homosexuality in other series of twins. The largest and best known study is that of Kallmann (*75*). He reported 100% concordance in 37 adequately investigated MZ pairs. The corresponding rate of 12% in 26 DZ pairs was considerably lower. Kallmann drew attention to the difficulties of investigating homosexual behavior. Of necessity he had to rely upon the sometimes reluctant aid given by psychiatric, correctional, and charitable agencies and by contacts with the clandestine homosexual world. Such sources may have made it more difficult for him to study co-twins who were normal than those who were homosexual. Further, he tried to restrict his index cases to persons who were predominantly or exclusively homosexual and who were over the age of 30. For these reasons Kallmann later (*128*)[2] regarded as a "statistical artifact" the 100% concordance rate in MZ twins. In 1953 (*78*) he reported a pair of MZ twins in which one twin was schizophrenic and homosexual and the other neither schizophrenic nor homosexual.

Earlier, in a series of criminal twins, Lange (*93*) found two who were homosexual. In one pair both MZ twins were homosexual, in the other pair one twin only. In the latter pair the homosexual twin had been brain damaged. Sanders (*134*) reported concordance in five of six male MZ pairs. The only DZ pair was discordant. The fact that only one DZ pair was reported raises doubts as to whether the sample was representative. Habel (*52*) found concordance in three of five MZ pairs and in none of five DZ pairs. The homosexual index twins had been found in a German prison population. He drew a distinction between "genuine" homosexuality and "pseudohomosexuality."

Koch (*83*), in the course of a good recent review of the topic, reported his own findings as regards homosexuality when he followed up, after 25 years, 495 pairs of nonpsychiatric, nondelinquent German twins. In this unselected series he found one female MZ and one male DZ twin who were homosexual, both pairs being discordant in this respect. The two male twins in Parker's London series (*121*), which was

---

2. Page 259 of the original article, page 29 in the present book.

based on the Maudsley Hospital Twin Register, 1959-1961, form part of the wider series to be reported in the present paper.

Besides the above series of twins, single discordant pairs of male MZ twins have been selected for special investigation by Rainer et al. (*128*) and Klintworth (*82*).

Though Kallmann's study overestimated the resemblance generally found in MZ pairs, it appears from the literature that MZ twins are significantly more often alike as regards male homosexuality than are DZ pairs. There is therefore prima facie evidence of the relevance of genetic factors. An alternative explanation, namely that monozygotic twinship itself predisposes to homosexuality, will be discussed later.

The Maudsley Twin Register

Since 1948, all patients admitted to the outpatient or inpatient services at the Maudsley Hospital, London, have been asked whether they are one of twins. All such twins ascertained who have twin partners of the same sex are enrolled on the Maudsley Twin Register, which is maintained by the Psychiatric Genetics Research Unit. The twin pairs are then further investigated by unit research workers. It should be emphasized that the series of twins is unselected as regards concordance and zygosity. Diagnostically, the probands appear representative of Maudsley patients as a whole. The Hospital Triennial Reports (*56*) and more detailed analyses made in the unit (*47*) have not shown an excess of twins or a relative excess of MZ over DZ pairs. The register has supplied material for several studies of twin pairs in various diagnostic groups (*121,47,122,144*) as described by Shields (*137*).

This report covers the male homosexual twins on the register as of July 31, 1966. The proband twins were examined as psychiatric patients. They and their co-twins were further assessed at various times through personal interviews and also, latterly, by means of psychological tests of intelligence (Dominoes; Mill Hill Vocabulary Scale, Senior) and personality (mostly the Maudsley Personality Inventory [MPI]). Usually supplementary information from doctors, hospitals, family members, or other such sources was obtained. Blood samples and fingerprints were taken if needed to establish the zygosity of the twins.

One of the subjects entering this series was from the unusual family mentioned above. Before considering the series as a whole, we will present this family.

The Family

The family had its roots in a notoriously poverty stricken area of a large city. The father and mother, both white and nominally Protestant, grew up, married, and established their own home in the same area. There were no twins in the family of either. At the time of their marriage, the father was a 22-year-old dock laborer, the mother 21 and a shop girl. Over the next 20 years they had 14 children, all of whom survived. The age and sex composition of the family is presented in Table 1.

TABLE 1. - *The Family*

	Age	Sex	Age at Marriage	Children	Occupation	Psychiatric Disorders
Father	77	M	22	14	Dock laborer, ret.	Alcoholic, sociopath, severe
Mother	76	F	21	14	Housewife	Passive personality, moderate
Sibship						
1	54	F	26	1	Family business	None
2A*	52	M	24	3	Typesetter	None
Twins						
2B	52	M	23	1	Machinist	None
3	49	M	27	2	Foreman, factory	None
4	46	M	23	2	Harbor pilot	None
5	44	F	24	2	Family business	Refused interview, considered normal
6	43	M	30	3	Foreman stagehand	None
7A	40	M	--	--	Cruise director	Homosexual; depression, mild
Twins						
7B	40	M	--	--	Headwaiter	Homosexual; depression, moderate

8	39	F	25	2	Housewife (husband PhD scientist)	Depression, severe
9A**	37	M	--	--	Record librarian	Homosexual; depression, moderate
Twins						
9B	37	M	--	--	Plumber,self-employed	Homosexual; depression, mild
10	35	M	25	2	Truck driver, small contractor	None
11	34	M	23	2	Route salesman	None

* The A twin was the first born in each pair
** Proband

The father, a heavy drinker, worked irregularly as a casual laborer on the waterfront. The mother remained in the home. The family was poor and was usually partially dependent on the rudimentary social services of the day.

After 25 years of marriage, the father was forced out of the home by the two oldest boys who were bolstered by social service agencies and finally the police and courts. None of the family members had further contact with him and indeed, most were not sure if he was alive or dead.

After the father left, the mother maintained the home and has remained in close contact with the children. However, the family was completely disrupted by World War II. The older children went into the armed services or war work and the younger were evacuated to foster families in rural areas in order to escape aerial bombing (as were most youngsters in the community).

After the war, the family reassembled in the same city; but by this time most of the older children had established their own homes and the younger ones were to do so within a few years. Later on, 9A moved to the London area.

Methods

The father, mother, and 13 of the 14 sibs were interviewed by a psychiatrist (L.L.H.) for at least one hour.   Each of the twins was interviewed at least twice.   Sufficient rapport was established with all these persons, except the mother, to allow questions regarding sexual activity and inclinations.   Excepting 2B who refused to complete printed tests or be fingerprinted but who did cooperate in all other ways, the twins were investigated according to the standard procedure described above.

Zygosity and Laboratory Findings. – The zygosity of the twins was determined by inspection and interpair resemblance in fingerprints, blood groups, and plasma proteins.   There was nothing in the appearance of the twins to suggest that any of the pairs was dizygotic, and the blood chemistry determinations revealed no intrapair differences in any of the 16 established genetic polymorphisms (*124*) that were investigated in the family.   At ten loci the parents and their children were identical – the genes involved did not segregate.   The findings with respect to the six independent polymorphisms in which the genes did segregate are displayed in Table 2.   These segregating genes, together with information from the fingerprints, allow calculation of the probability of the twins being MZ or DZ.   The steps in this calculation are shown in Table 3, following the method of Smith and Penrose (*146*). The odds assigned to likeness in the blood group (*126*) and plasma protein systems (*57*) were derived from known genetic ratios, while the relative chance of observed differences in the fingerprints was calculated by the method of Slater (*143*).   The final probability of monozygosity was: 2A and B, 0.991; 7A and B, 0.999; and 9A and B, 0.999.

TABLE 2. - *Segregating Genetic Polymorphisms**

	Sex	ABO	MNS	Rh	Duffy	Haptoglobin	Phospho-glucomutase
			Blood Groups			Plasma Proteins	
Father	M	B	MsMs	R1r	a-b+	2-1	2-1
Mother	F	O	MSNs	R1r	a+b+	2-2	2-1
Children							
1	F	O	MSMs	R1r	a+b+	2-1	2
2A & 2B	M	B	MSMs	rr	a+b+	2-2**	1
3	M	O	MsNs	rr	a+b+	2-1	1
4	M	B	MSMs	R1r	a-b+	2-2	2-1
5	F	B***	-	rr***	-	-	-
6	M	B	MSMs	R1r	a-b+	2-1	2-1
7A & 7B	M	B	MSMs	R1r	a+b+	2-1	1
8	F	O	MSMs	R1R1	a+b+	2-2	2
9A & 9B	M	O	MSMs	R1r	a-b+	2-2	2-1
10	M	B	MSMs	R1r	a+b+	2-2	2
11	M	B	MSMs	rr	a+b+	2-1	2-1

* Both parents and all sibs were: P_1, Lu(a-), K-, Le(a+b-), Xg(a+), Do(a+),
transferrin C, red blood cell acid phosphatase B, 6-phosphogluconate dehydrogenase A
and adenylate kinase 1.
** 2A only. No haptoglobin was detected in 2B's sample.
*** Stated by subject.
Antisera used: Anti-A, -A$_1$, -B, anti-A+B, anti-M, -N, -S, -s, anti-P$_1$, anti-C, -c^w,
-c, -D, -E, -e, anti-Lu^a, anti-K, anti-Le^a, -Le^b, anti-Fy^a-Fy^b, anti-Xg^a, anti-Do^a.

A karotype was prepared from a white blood cell (WBC) culture
from 7A and was normal. It was highly unlikely that any of the children

were illegitimate. There was no indication of any relationship between the investigated genetic polymorphisms and twinning, homosexuality, or enuresis.

TABLE 3. - *Zygosity Probability Calculation**

1. *Relative odds of dizygosity (DZ:MZ)*			
In twins in general			
Initial odds (70:30)	2.3333	2.3333	2.3333
Like-sexed twins(0.5:1)	0.5	0.5	0.5
In twins with observed resemblance in fingerprints			
(from Slater (*143*), 1963)	-	0.0173	0.0322
In this family, given twin A of pair:			
Twins alike in ABO blood groups	0.5	0.5	0.5
Twins alike in MNS blood groups	0.5	0.5	0.5
Twins alike in Rh blood groups	0.25	0.5	0.5
Twins alike in Duffy blood groups	0.5	0.5	0.5
Twins alike in Haptoglobin	-	0.5	0.5
Twins alike in Phosphoglucomutase	0.25	0.5	0.5

Product of independent odds (total relative chance,			
pD, in Smith-Penrose terminology)	0.00912	0.000158	0.000685
2. *Probabilities (total chance, in Smith-Penrose*			
terminology):			
That twins are dizygotic pD/(1 + pD)	0.00904	0.000158	0.000587
That twins are monozygotic 1/(1 + pD)	0.991	0.999	0.999

* Based on the method of Smith and Penrose (*146*).

Interview Results

The Father. — This man was unanimously condemned by his wife and children. He drank heavily two or three nights per week and as often would beat the mother severely. The children were infrequently beaten but were often punished with unreasonable severity; i.e., being tied to a bed for several hours. They were also threatened with even severer punishment, sometimes death. One son (No. 6), recalled father pinning him in a corner with a chair, taking out a knife and saying, "I am going to kill you — right now." Several of his children reported that they still felt fearful when talking about him, recalled hiding from him, even sleeping out all night in order to avoid him.

When interviewed, he was 77 years old, living alone in one cluttered room, and supported by a pension. He felt that he had been unjustly deserted by his family. His wife had manipulated him by threatening suicide whenever disagreements arose. Her lack of cooperation had driven him to heavy drinking and occasionally he had been forced to handle her roughly. Mention of his children evoked no evidence of feeling or interest. No evidence of significant cerebral impairment was noted. He denied homosexual experiences.

The Mother. – This woman was 76 years old when interviewed. She was highly regarded by her children, although several suspected that she had exaggerated the injuries she received from her husband and a succession of minor ailments. When interviewed, she appeared ill at ease and gave "yes-no" answers to most questions. She had remained with her husband because of her fear – "he could always find me" – and only took a firm stand when her oldest sons were able to protect her. She had often felt like committing suicide and threatened her husband with this. She felt that she had insufficent time to spend with her children because there were so many. However, she loved them all from the time they were born, had no particular favorite, and none were especially troublesome. All the children were dressed and reared in accordance with their biologic sex. She controlled the children by exhortations: she could not bring herself to spank them. Her children felt that she was a warm, loving woman who had some minor failings, but who did her best in the most difficult circumstances.

The Heterosexual Children. – All of these persons described themselves as being unhappy as children, citing the father's cruelty and the family's poverty. Several (No. 3, 4, 8, and 10) were enuretic until early adolescence. As the family grew, considerable responsibility for the younger children was assumed by those who were older. One of the older twins (2A) had been deliberately assuming the role of father to the seven youngest children during the last year his father was in the home. He is still affectionately referred to as "Pa." His twin carried out more feminine chores in the home, such as shopping and child care. Both 2A and his twin have been exclusively heterosexual and there was no evidence of serious psychiatric disorder.

One woman (No. 5) refused the interview, pleading lack of time. (This was probably realistic.) She was married and working successfully. Some information was obtained through telephone contact. She was regarded as psychiatrically normal.

Another woman (No. 8) had suffered intermittent depressions. After her last pregnancy (seven years past), she felt depressed with prominent hypochondrical symptoms and seriously considered suicide. When interviewed, she felt dissatisfied with her role as housewife in which she was "vegetating."

Homosexual Twin Pair 7A and 7B. – These twins were 40 when interviewed. Both held junior executive positions in entertainment and recreation business.

Following a normal gestation period, these twins developed normally in relation to the usual landmarks. The eldest, 7A (by 20 minutes) and the heaviest (5¾ lb, one quarter pound heavier) was the more active and aggressive. From an early age, the twins preferred to play separately and were seldom in each other's company. However, A added that they stuck together in any adverse circumstance. Like their siblings, they remember their early years as unhappy, because of poverty and fear of their father. Both describe their mother as "wonderful," but B felt she did not have enough time for them. Neither felt they were overprotected or specially treated in any way. Both were enuretic for many years, A to age 10, B to age 12. From ages 8 to 10, they were in separate homes. B remained with the mother, while A lived with a neighboring family, who had taken a liking to him. A remembers these two years as being especially happy. During this period, B began secretly donning female clothing and applying mascara and lipstick. This practice gave him a "thrill" and continued for about a year. During a six-month period, starting at about 12 years, B began to have vivid dreams of himself in the mother-wife role in a family. His husband was a powerful, unrecognizable man, who periodically "enveloped" him. His twin denied corresponding experiences.

By age 14, when they left school, both realized that they were unlike other boys. They disliked rough games, were effeminate in speech and gesture, felt neutral toward females, and positively attracted toward males. B, still slightly smaller and now the more effeminate, began working as a waiter in a nightclub. Shortly afterward, he began a series of casual homosexual encounters. He was rejected for military service because he acknowledged his homosexuality. His twin had no overt sexual activity until he entered the navy at age 17. After a few brief homosexual affairs and two unsuccessful attempts at heterosexual relations, A developed an intense attachment for a fellow sailor, who has lived with him as his homosexual partner for 20 years. He felt that this prolonged affair was exactly analogous to heterosexual marriage. A acknowledged episodes of moderate depression attributed to fear of being exposed as a homosexual and regret that he would never have a family and children. Otherwise, he felt quite content with his life.

B also had only one homosexual partner, whom he met during the period when his twin was in the navy, and with whom he has lived ever since. However, B sometimes finds pickup partners at homosexual parties. Like his twin, B has been subject to depressions and he cited the same reasons. However, B has been more severely affected. At age 35, he sought psychiatric treatment and attended a few group meetings. He was regarded as suffering from an anxiety state with secondary autonomic accompaniment: he did not reveal his homosexuality. Although he has never felt as if he might commit suicide, he would welcome some fatal calamity.

The strikingly similar pattern of homosexual behavior developed in these twins entirely independently. During the time period when they found their separate partners, A was in the navy. He did not return home during this period and he and his twin did not exchange a single letter. Each was ignorant of his twin's homosexuality until about ten years after A's navy service when they confided in each other.

The interviews with these twins elicited no evidence of psychiatric disorder other than homosexuality although both had histories of depression. Both had learned to disguise their feminine mannerisms through strenuous effort, A more successfully than B. Both denied sexual contact or feeling toward their co-twin. They were of high normal intelligence with A slightly the brighter. A, with a score of 24, was considerably less neurotic than B, who scored 36 on the MPI.

Homosexual Twin Pair 9A and 9B. – These younger twins were 37 when interviewed. Their birth and early developmental history were unremarkable. Although their exact birth weights were unknown, their mother thought they were about 6 lb and nearly equal in weight. Through their early years, they came to avoid each other's company because, according to A, "We were shown off together, were expected to be together, and we resented this."

The twins lived in the family home until age 10, when they were evacuated to different foster homes at the start of World War II. Up to this time, and for another year, both twins were enuretic.

During the period in the foster family, A was befriended by a 35-year-old man, who lived in the home. This man was "kind" and "gentle," and was "the only father I had ever known." His benefactor seduced A and the two began a homosexual affair which continued for six months. During the same period, his twin was living in a nearby home with several other boys. He was forced into homosexual acts by some of the older boys.

After four years in foster homes, the twins returned to their mother and discontinued all sexual practices except masturbation. Neither knew of the other's homosexuality and, although both were suspicious, they were not certain at the time of this investigation.

At age 17, both went into military service and were posted to different overseas stations. Both resumed homosexual practices and both had sporadic heterosexual affairs, which neither found satisfactory. Of the pair, B was the more active heterosexually and at age 33 was engaged to be married. He felt he could tolerate marriage and wanted children; however, he could not explain his periodic lack of sexual interest to his fiancee, nor his being so often out at night with men and he broke the engagement. He felt that he could not in good faith marry a normal woman, although he had not ruled out the possibility entirely. His twin's heterosexual activity had been almost entirely with prostitutes "to see if I could enjoy it." He derived little satisfaction from this and had stopped all contacts several years before.

This pair of twins had frequent homosexual relations with several partners. Both acted as fellators. A associated with casual pickups, many of whom he paid, while B had several men, "old friends," whom he "dated." Most of the latter men were married. Neither would consider living with a man as 7A and 7B did and both preferred nonhomosexual sex partners. Like their older twin brothers, this pair denied any sexual contact or feeling for each other and reported the idea as distasteful.

Both twins felt mildly depressed and anxious most of the time with occasional exacerbations. They separately ascribed these feelings to fear of exposure as a homosexual, and their inability to found a family. A was much the stronger in his expressions of depressed feelings and added that he often felt shame and disgust after a homosexual act. A sought psychiatric treatment for his homosexuality. At 36, after coming to London, he had a few psychotherapeutic interviews privately, then was referred to the Maudsley. He rejected the offer of aversion therapy. When seen for the present investigation six months later, there was no evidence of psychiatric disorder in either twin other than homosexuality with secondary depression. A had slightly more effeminate mannerisms than B, although neither was striking in this respect. However, when A was more obviously depressed and was seen at the Maudsley, he was described as very effeminate. Psychological tests show the twins to be in the bright normal range with B slightly more intelligent.

A, who had changed jobs several times, felt less successful vocationally than B. B found considerable satisfaction in his work.

Comments on the Family

The salient feature of this family's history is the concordance in sexual behavior of the three sets of MZ twins and especially the concordance of the two sets of homosexual twins. It is also notable that, in agreement with Slater's findings (*142*), the latter twins came late in the birth order and that the mother's age (35 for the first set) was relatively advanced. This evidence suggests a genetic vulnerability to homosexuality, possibly operating through fresh gene mutations or chromosomal errors. However, the findings can be interpreted otherwise and, taken alone, add little substantial knowledge. The following consideration of similarities and differences within and between the homosexual twins and their siblings is an attempt to slip between the horns of the sterile nature-nurture dilemma.

Homosexuals vs Other Sibs. – The environment in which the children were raised must be regarded as severely disruptive. Clearly the father was a heavy drinker, who brutalized the mother and inspired great fear in the children. Fear of their father characterizes a high proportion of homosexual men (*12,14*). There were 14 children and the nurture available from the mother was spread thinly. The family was poverty stricken, lived in a slum area, and the younger children were displaced because of war.

These major features of the environment did not change during the period when the children were growing up. All of the 14 sibs were at risk. If such an environment were predictable in producing adverse effects, it would be reasonable to postulate that the behavior of all the children would exhibit some evidence of psychological scarring. A continuum of behavioral disorder should be apparent. But the disability was, instead, discontinuous. Most of the children became successful adults. The homosexuality of the twins and threads of depression running through the histories of these same twins and their sister (No. 8) contrast sharply with the social effectiveness and apparent psychological health of the other nine siblings.

Two major postulates can be formed to account for the homosexuality of the twins:

(1) There must have been some special vulnerability, genetic or constitutional, in the affected persons which predisposed them to homosexuality. If such a vulnerability is admitted, the unfavorable environment may well have contributed to the final result. (2) The environment alone determined the homosexuality. This proposition cannot be proved on the basis of the evidence and cannot be disproved in principle. However, it is beset with difficulties. The same or closely related environmental factors would have to select out four persons – the two sets of homosexual twins – and leave the other children, including a third set of twins, untouched. Obvious environmental features, such as the fear-inspiring father, which common sense would depict as highly deleterious, would have to be relegated to non-

contributory or at most accessory etiologic roles because all of the children were exposed. Of course, it is possible that there existed in the family environment factors, which were so (apparently) trivial as to escape notice or leave ready memories with any of the informants, yet which were so selective, specific, and profound in effect as to determine homosexuality in only the affected persons. But this seems most unlikely.

Between Homosexual Twin Pairs. – There were major sociopsychological differences between the twin pairs. The pair 7A and 7B lived with permanent partners for whom they expressed strong affectional ties. They described their marriage as analogous to heterosexual marriage and were highly critical of "promiscuous" homosexuals. Their younger twin brothers had more heterosexual experience and had conducted their homosexual activities with temporary partners. They would not consider living with a man.

Since these twin pairs are brothers, it is likely that the same basic etiologic factor(s) produced the major deviation, i.e., homosexuality. If this is true, then the differences between the pairs, although striking, are attributable to modifying genes or life experiences, which are incidental to homosexuality per se. This gives support to the concept that the several types of homosexual behavior do not necessarily entail several primary etiologies.

Within Homosexual Twin Pairs. – These twins were not only concordant for homosexuality, but the members of each pair had developed modes of sexual behavior strikingly similar to each other. Furthermore, they did this while ignorant of their co-twin's homosexuality and, for 7A and 7B, while widely separated geographically. This finding echoes the report of Kallmann (75). But there were also major differences within the twin pairs and these could not be produced by environmental differences. 7B, always smaller, less robust, and less aggressive than his twin, was also the more effeminate and practiced transvestism briefly. He was more liable to depressions. Within the younger pair, 9A was more homosexual in orientation, yet less accepting of himself as a homosexual and more liable to depressions. He was also vocationally less successful than his twin.

The differences between 7A and 7B were lifelong and are reasonably well explained by the size and weight differences. Such differences and other related ones appear to be of major importance in normal MZ twins (138,154) and possibly in twins that are discordant for schizophrenia (123). The differences between 9A and 9B became apparent later in life and have increased. The seduction of B by an older man, who had treated him kindly and assumed a fatherly role when 9A's life was disrupted, is an experience considered of critical etiologic importance by East (*32*) and many others (*151,149A*). It is also from this point in time that the differences between the twin pair began to emerge. The seduction is most unlikely to have determined 9A's homosexuality because 9B, also homosexual, had no such experience. But it could well account for much of the intrapair difference and this is clearly of great importance. 9B had nearly married and had had considerable heterosexual experience, which he found mildly pleasurable. It is not unreasonable to suppose that he would have made a heterosexual adjustment of sorts given favorable circumstances. His twin exhibited no evidence of such a capability.

In summary, the evidence presented by this family, will not support either genetic or environmental determinism as an explanation of the homosexuality of the twin pairs. An etiology based on the interaction of these factors is required.

The Registry Study

We shall now report briefly on the other homosexual twin pairs on the register. Conclusions will be limited by smallness of numbers and by the fact that homosexuals referred to a psychiatric clinic cannot be assumed to be representative of all homosexuals. Similar objections can be raised to most clinical studies of homosexuality.

We have set out in Table 4 the salient facts relating to all 12 male twins on the register who had a primary or secondary diagnosis of homosexuality and whose MZ or male DZ twins had passed the age of 15 when last heard of. A 13th case, from overseas, had to be omitted for lack of information. The zygosity of the listed pairs is reasonably secure and is supported by blood groups in all MZ and in four DZ pairs. The remaining three DZ pairs differ clearly in appearance, including hair color.

TABLE 4. - *Homosexuals on Psychiatric Clinic Twin Register*

No.	Age, Last Info MA* Place in Sibship**	Proband Sexual History	Notable Background Features: Other Abnormality	Co-Twin
		MZ Pairs		
1	Age,40 MA,45 Twins,5/5	At 10, priest interfered with his private parts. Homosexual practices by 24.At 30 inpatient(IP), homosexuality.Single.	Onset of *schizophrenia* at 14.First hospitalization at 17.In state of good remission when hospitalized for homo problems.Later some deterioration.	Single.No homo practices.Onset of *schizophrenia* at 29.*Delusion of sex change* at at 30.*Indecent exposure* at 34. Longer hospitalization than proband.
2**	Age,29 MA,39 Twins,2/2	Regular homo activity from adolescence.Outpatient at 26.	Though not dressed as a girl or given a feminine name, proband (but not co-twin) was thought to have been treated by mother, who wanted a girl, in some ways as if he were one. No other abnormality.	Married,2 children.Normal.
3	Age,43 MA,35 Twins,3/4	Homo inclinations from early age & intermittent practice.IP at 43, illness precipitated by being teased on account of effeminacy.Single.	Overconscientious,liable to attacks of anxiety & depression.*Depressive episode with delusions* at 43,diagnosed reactive depression,homo.	Single.*Practicing homo* from early age.Personality as proband.At 33 IP,*depression with psychotic symptoms*,good recovery.

4***	Age,37 MA,39 Twins,9/11	Homo.Single,OP at 36.	Depression secondary to homo.	Single.Homo. Mild,untreated secondary de- pression.
5	Age,22 MA,31 Twins,1/1	Homo from adolescence. OP at 22.Single.	Mother died when twins 4;brought up by grandmother,got on indifferently with father.No psychiatric abnormality.	Single.Hetero- sexual activ- ity.No evidence latent homo.

DZ Pairs

1	Age,33 MA,31 Twins,2/2	First aware of homo inclinations at 21.OP at 26 with worry over homo, diagnosed.Inadequate psychopath with homo tendencies.Later, con- firmed homo practices. Single.	Brought up in poor working-class district. Unhappy home:much quar- reling between parents, father drinker,mother shrill-voiced,overpower- ing in manner,elder sister epileptic,getting divorce.At 21,OP,*anxiety attacks,*fears of impend- ing death, somatic symptoms of anxiety, depressed following change of job.	Single.Dress designer.At 26 engaged to dominant girl, homo fears. Later breaks engagement, mixes in homo circles,*regards himself as homo.*No psych illness
2	Age,45 MA,32	Regular homo practices since 20.OP at 37.	None.	Married,1 child.Normal.
3	Age,39	Homo feelings from 9; practices from 14.At 28 court charge.At 31 OP. Single.	None.	Single.In religious or- der requiring celibacy.No overt homo.? Mild reactive depression when studying.

4	Age,22/26 MA,25 Twins,1/1	Homo practices from 14. In "care and protection" for this at 16,IP at 17, diag homo,immature personality.Continued homo activities.Single.	Unstable background:neglected by mother,parents divorced.*Unstable personality:* frequently on probation for larceny;many changes of job;at least 11 suicidal attempts,4 of them serious,and eventually committed suicide (overdose) at 22.	Age 26.Married, does not want responsibility of children.As adolescent, much casual hetero activity.Since 18,OP for aggressive behavior,secondary anxiety? malingering.Usually regarded as *psychopath.*
5	Age,20 MA,29 Twins,1/1	Homo practices from 12, also some transvestism. In court at 16,then OP, diag homo.Later gets girl friend (?)	Father rejecting;mother has disseminated sclerosis.At OP secondary diagnosis of psychopath(larceny,absenteeism, unrealistic attitudes,bad relations with father).On follow-up behavior said to be improved.	Single.No homo inclinations. Normal.
6$	Age,38 MA,34 Twins,1/3	Fetishism from 13;masochism,first of three arrests at 26.Psychoanalysis at 29,OP at 34,sexual perversion.Forced marriage to fellow patient,1 child.	Father eccentric,paranoid.Highly intelligent.Many personality & occupational problems resulting in lowering of occupation-status (sociopathic).	Married at 34.Successful.No homo or psychiat illness.
7	Age,21 MA,35 Twins,4/4	Homo from 14.OP at 20. Single.	Overpossessive mother (case referred for social work).No psychiatric abnormality.	Single.No homo inclinations. Normal.

* Mother's age at birth of twins.
** Previously reported by Parker (*121*) (case A).
*** The proband for the large family reported above.
**** In terms of mother's effective pregnancies.
$ Previously reported by Parker (*121*) (case B).

Intrapair Resemblance as to Homosexuality. – In two of five MZ pairs (MZ 3 and 4), both twins were clearly homosexual. In a third pair (MZ 1) the co-twin had what may have been a related sexual deviation (delusion of sex change, exposed himself). Both these latter twins were schizophrenic, and in each the sexual deviation only became manifest after onset of the psychosis. For a number of years the picture in MZ 1 was similar to that of the case described by Kallmann and referred to above (*78*). The concordance rate, if one wishes to calculate it on such small numbers, is between 40% and 60% depending on how one deals with MZ 1.

Two MZ co-twins were heterosexual. In one of these (MZ 2, case A of Parker (*121*)), the difference in sexual behavior was consistent with differences in the attitude of the mother. This case shows that discordance is not restricted to the less confirmed type of homosexuality. In the other discordant pair (MZ 5) we were unable to discover any reason for the apparently spontaneous development at adolescence of homosexual interests and behavior in one twin only. Though the proband had for some time been on poorer terms with his father than was his co-twin, this could as easily have been the consequence of his effeminacy as a critical environmental factor accounting for the differences between the twins.

Turning to the 7 DZ pairs, one (DZ 1) is probably concordant for homosexuality, though there is no direct evidence of physical relations in the case of the co-twin. Diagnosing the histories of pair DZ 1 independently of one another and in ignorance of zygosity, Dr. Eliot Slater in an earlier study (*139*) classified both twins as homosexuals. This would give a concordance rate of 14%. Of the six nonhomosexual DZ co-twins, three are married. The ages of those who have so far never married are 20, 21, and 39. In the last case (DZ 3) one might speculate about a latent homosexuality.

The tendency shown in the present sample, as in cases from the literature, is thus for concordance and discordance to occur about equally frequently in MZ pairs, given that one of them is homosexual, while concordance is less frequent in DZ pairs.

Homosexuality among the sibs, as opposed to the twins, of the 12 probands, was found only in case MZ 4. Holemon and Winokur (*67*) reported that out of 40 homosexuals, 2 had a homosexual sib.

Other Psychiatric Conditions. – Since this is a series of twins where one was seen at a psychiatric hospital, cases of major psychiatric disorder may be mentioned. Besides the schizophrenic twins of pair MZ 1, there was a second MZ pair (MZ 3) where the proband had a severe depression requiring hospitalization. Here both twins seem to have had a tendency to affective disorder independent of homosexuality. In general, the presence or absence of other diagnosed psychiatric conditions in the MZ probands does not appear to account for the resemblance in homosexuality.

Four DZ probands had, in varying degrees, unstable or inadequate personalities which contributed to their referral to the Maudsley Hospital; one of them (DZ 4), from a disturbed home background, had a co-twin who was also psychiatrically abnormal but was heterosexual.

Frequency of Homosexuality
in Twins per se

It has been argued that the tendency for MZ twins to be more alike than DZ twins in homosexuality is related not so much to genetic factors as to problems of sexual identification connected with being a monozygotic twin, which in turn predispose towards homosexuality *(96,111)*. It could indeed be pointed out (though not, we think, with justification) that in the sibship reported in the first part of our paper four out of six males who were twins were also homosexual, while this was so in none of the five males who were singly born. We may therefore ask: Does the Maudsley Twin Register reveal a relative excess of homosexuality in MZ as compared with DZ twins? The 5 MZ homosexuals come from 82 MZ or probably MZ adult male twins on the Register (6.1%), and the 7 DZ homosexuals from 97 (7.2%). These findings do not support the hypothesis which associates monozygosity with homosexuality.

It is harder to say precisely whether the incidence of homosexuality in members of same-sexed male twins is greater than in the parent Maudsley population, since there are features about the way in which the hospital statistics are compiled which make comparison with our twin series difficult. However, a count of diagnostic punched cards (one card for each discharge) for the period 1952-1957 was previously made by one of us (J.S.); and this showed that a primary diagnosis of 320.6 (sexual deviation) was made in the case of patients who were twins of *any* kind in a proportion very close to that made in all patients (3.2% and 3.1% respectively). As already noted the ratio of twins to non-twins is about the same in the Maudsley as in the general population.

A follow-up of 27 pairs of normal London male twins (i. e., 54 individuals) at an age between 22 and 25 revealed none that were homosexual (Harrison and Shields, unpublished data). The findings are similar to those of the much larger prospective study of normal German twins by Koch (*83*), which discovered only one male homosexual twin.

There therefore appears to be no good evidence from the present material or from other work for supposing that twins have a high risk of being homosexual.

Summary

An unusual family with a sibship of 14 has been investigated clinically and in respect of 16 genetic polymorphisms (blood groups and plasma proteins). Among the sibs were three pairs of male monozygotic twins, in two of which both twins were homosexual and in the third both heterosexual. No environmental factors could be detected which differentiated the homosexual from the heterosexual sibs. All grew up in what must be regarded as a severely disruptive environment, yet most of the children were successful adults. Clinical differences between the two homosexual pairs and differences within each of them have been discussed. An etiology based on the interaction of genetic and environmental factors is required to explain the findings.

The above family came to notice through the study of a consecutive series of twins. To date, 12 pairs of male twins in which one or both is homosexual have been recorded on a register of all twins attending a psychiatric clinic. These pairs have been described briefly and the literature reviewed. There is no evidence that monozygotic twins per se are particularly prone to homosexuality. The tendency is for concordance to be incomplete in series of MZ twins but to be higher than in corresponding DZ twins, a finding which once again points to the importance of both genetic and environmental causes.

Monozygotic Twins Discordant for Homosexuality: Report of a Pair and Significance of the Phenomenon

Bernard Zuger[1]

In view of the high concordance rate for homosexuality in monozygotic twins (75,61), instances of discordance are of special interest. Their occurrence has contributed to the controversy over the genetic versus the environmental causation of homosexuality. In this report, I will add another such instance and will review some early medical and behavioral factors found in this pair of twins and eight others drawn from the English language literature. It will be argued that

1. From the Department of Psychiatry, New York School of Medicine, New York, N.Y., and the Children's Psychiatric Clinic, Greenwich Hospital, Greenwich, Conn.

Bernard Zuger, M.D.: Associate Clinical Professor, Department of Psychiatry, New York University School of Medicine, New York, N.Y., and Psychiatrist, Children's Psychiatric Clinic, Greenwich Hospital, Greenwich, Conn.

Supported in part by a grant from the Greenwich Health Association, Greenwich, Conn.

Reprint requests should be addressed to Bernard Zuger, M.D., New York University Medical Center, Department of Psychiatry, 550 First Avenue, New York, N.Y. 10016.

ACKNOWLEDGEMENTS

The blood grouping was done in the serology laboratory of Dr. Alexander S. Wiener of the New York City Medical Examiner's Office and the New York University School of Medicine. Dr. Weiner also made the zygosity calculations.

The dermatoglyphic prints were analyzed by Dr. Lawrence R. Shapiro, Director of Cytogenetics at Letchworth Village, Thiells, N.Y.

Dr. Robert Schwimmer of Greenwich, Conn. first saw the patients and made the study possible.

the evidence from these monozygotic twins does not lend support to the environmental theory of the causation of homosexuality.

Case History

The twins were first brought to my attention, when they were 20 years of age, by their family doctor, who was treating the heterosexual twin for infectious hepatitis. The homosexual twin was undergoing a psychotic episode, had attempted suicide, and had been hospitalized. He was being seen by another psychiatrist. Both twins and their parents were subsequently seen by me, but the questioning of the homosexual twin had to be limited because of his fragile psychologic state. The others were fully cooperative.

Zygosity was determined in several ways. Blood grouping gave the following results.

	A-B-O	M-N	Kell	Rh-Hr
Father	A_1B	MN	k	Rh_1rh
Mother	O	MN	k	Rh_1rh
First twin	B	MN	k	Rh_1Rh_1
Second twin	B	MN	k	Rh_1Rh_1

According to the calculations of Wiener and Leff (*163*), the odds that the like-sexed twins were monozygotic were 100:3 or about 33 to 1.

Dermatoglyphic analysis revealed a total finger ridge count of 58 for the heterosexual twin and 56 for the homosexual twin. With a difference of 2, the probability of the twins being monozygotic was 73% - 77%, according to the probability tables of Holt (*68*). The palms showed no interdigital, thenar, or hypothenar patterns in either of the twins. The axial triradii were in the t + t' positions with ulnar deviation on the right and in the t position on the left for the heterosexual twin, and in the t + t' positions with deviation bilaterally for the homosexual twin.

The clinical characteristics of the twins, such as the color of hair and eyes and the difficulty with which they were told apart as infants, were also used to determine their zygosity according to the method of Cohen *et al.* (*23*) This gave an index of 35.9, the discriminatory point being 26.7, above which the likelihood of embryonic origin was monozygotic and below which, dizygotic.

In photographs taken at 6 months and at 1 year of age the twins appeared identical. One of the twins remembered being taken as identical by strangers up to about 7 years of age, but being differentiated after that. Both are nearsighted and wear glasses. Neither is colorblind, and both are right-handed.

The twins were the product of the mother's second pregnancy, being preceded by a male sibling 4 years older and followed by a male sibling 13 years younger. They were wanted by both parents, who denied having any sex preferences. Neither of the twins was named after their father, but both were given distinctly masculine names. Except for an X-ray 3 weeks before term, pregnancy and delivery were uneventful. The twin who later became homosexual was first-born and weighed 2977 gm. He was followed immediately by the heterosexual co-twin who weighed 3062 gm. The mother thought they were identical but wondered whether she might have been influenced by what the pediatrician told her. The father and strangers had difficulty in telling them apart.

The neonatal period in the noneffeminate boy was highlighted by his developing symptoms of congenital pyloric stenosis, for which the Ramstedt operation was done. The homosexual twin remained well. They were not breast fed.

The heterosexual twin may have walked somewhat earlier than his co-twin, but both started talking at the same time, talking to each other "in their own language" a little later.

During childhood, the effeminate twin was considered more sickly than his co-twin. The former was subjected to a tonsillectomy at 2 years of age, the latter not until 8 years of age. Both contracted measles at 3-4 years of age, during which the effeminate boy went through an episode of high fever with twitching and jerking of the extremities.

When the effeminate boy was 3-4 years of age, the mother began to notice "little feminine characteristics" about him, which were apparently also noticed by his brothers, for they began to "pick" on him. At about 5 years of age the kindergarten teacher referred to him as an "effeminate little boy" and urged treatment. He preferred to be with his mother rather than with his father, brothers, or other boys. He played with dolls and showed no interest in boys' games or sports, preferring "artistic" and musical pursuits and acting. His gestures were effeminate. He had few friends and was considered a "loner." This was in marked contrast to his twin brother who was outgoing, a ringleader, interested in boys' games and sports, and did carpentry for a hobby.

The father's employment necessitated considerable travel and up to the time when the twins were about 8 years of age, he was frequently away during the week, returning home for the weekend. Subsequently, he had longer assignments in the United States and abroad and was accompanied by his family. The twins, therefore, attended several schools. They did well, but at about 13 years of age, the effeminate boy's grades began to fall off and he required help with some subjects. In high school, both boys ranked in the upper fifth percentile, though the effeminate boy lagged behind in math. His mannerisms were then described by his teacher as extremely effeminate, resembling a girl's in speech and movement. He continued his interests in music and acting. His brother was active in athletics and was masculine in appearance and voice.

Toward the end of high school and in the first year of college, the effeminate boy began "experimenting" with both sexes. At one time a girl accused him of making her pregnant, but this turned out not to be the case. He also began having "affairs" with men, one of several months' duration whom he spoke of "marrying." It was at about this time that he became depressed, developed visual and auditory hallucinations, and attempted suicide. He was then hospitalized.

The noneffeminate boy had shown some proneness to anxiety (as did the mother and other siblings), manifested early by fright on a chair lift and later by fear of heights and of dying. He was more intense and competitive than his co-twin. He denied ever experiencing any attraction to boys or men or having any sexual relations with them. He also denied any mutual masturbation with his co-twin. He was attracted to girls in high school and had dates but no sex relations until the first year in college. For a short period he was fearful that he might become like his brother because he was his identical co-twin. At 23 years of age, he became engaged to a girl he had met in college and subsequently married her.

The mother and the father were 25 and 29 years of age, respectively, when the twins were born. Both twins, as well as the older sibling, were closer to the mother than to the father, partly because he was away much of the time during the early years. The noneffeminate twin spoke about his relationship with his mother as a good and open one and characterized the brother's as one requiring "covering up" and "doctoring."

The mother had finished three years of college when she left to get married. She was socially active and was consulted by friends for their problems. She was a conscientious housekeeper. The mother's own family consisted of one brother and two nieces and one nephew who showed no evidence of sexual deviations.

The father was described by the mother as gentle and loving and as being the dominant member of the family. Both she and the noneffeminate twin felt that he had not spent enough time with them, though he had been generous with gifts. The same son expressed "respect" for his father but thought of him as "too authoritative," "stoic," and "too logical." He seemed preoccupied with business and played golf instead of playing with his boys or "communicating" with his famiily. The son, however, did remember his father "reinforcing" him when playing football or doing his carpentry, something he could not do for the effeminate co-twin from whom he had become distant because he was not "masculine." The mother independently gave a similar version of the father's reactions.

The father was professionally trained and successful. He was one of four children with eight nieces and nephews who, to his knowledge, showed no sexual deviations.

When seen together, the parents appeared open and outgoing. From all the evidence available, there was justification in rating the marriage a good one.

Discussion

The possibility that the twins are dizygotic is small and made more unlikely by the corroborative evidence from the different tests for zygosity, though cannot be absolutely ruled out. Other explanations for the discordance in sex orientation would seem to be more likely, namely, a congenital difference in development other than genetic, pre-, para-, or postnatal factors, and differential familial environmental influences.

Clues for these possibilities were sought in eight twin monozygotic pairs, discordant for homosexuality, gathered from the English language literature, which represented all the cases reported that made any contribution to the data being sought no matter how small; they were otherwise nonselective. These and the pair reported here are summarized in Tables 1-4 (*128,82,121,27,50*).

Eight of the nine twin pairs with data were products of the first or second pregnancy, slightly more of the second than the first pregnancy. This is in line with what has been found for single-born children with early effeminate behavior, whom the homosexual twins resemble in early onset and syptomatology, as indicated below.

The data on the kinds of birth experienced by the twins, their birth order, and birth weights are either too scant or not sufficiently different for such a small series to be significant. There were more serious infectious illnesses in the male homosexual twins than in their co-twins. Here, too, the cases are too few in number to warrant any conclusions.

What the data in Tables 1 and 2 do indicate is that major and minor differences of a physical and mental nature may be experienced by monozygotic twins. For instance, in the twin pair reported here, only the heterosexual boy suffered from congenital pyloric stenosis. Yet congenital pyloric stenosis is 80 times more prevalent in monozygotic twins of probands than in the general population, according to Carter (*21*), who also reports its occurrence in one of a pair of "probably" monozygotic twin brothers (*22*). The discordance does not alter the fact that congenital pyloric stenosis has a strong genetic predilection. Twinning as such, regardless of zygosity, has its own "perturbations" (e.g., crowding, circulatory complications) as indicated clinically, for instance, in the greater number of cases of "minimal brain dysfunction" among twins than in a comparable group of nontwins (*120*). Boklage (*15*) has argued evidentially for the possibility of an embryonic factor apart from a genetic one to explain differences in monozygotic twins. From the behavioral side, Wilson and Brown (*168*) have pointed out that even where there are significant differences in concordance rates for certain behaviors between monozygotic and dizygotic twins, the intermonozygotic concordance may be far from complete.

Table 1. Birth and Other Factors in Male Monozygotic Twins Discordant for Homosexuality

			Heterosexual Twin				Homosexual Twin					
Case No.	Age First Seen (yr)	Gravid Order	Birth	Twin Birth Order	Birth Weight (gm)	Medical and Other Factors	Birth	Twin Birth Order	Birth Weight (gm)	Age Effeminate Symptoms Noted (yr)	Medical and Other Factors	Reference
1	29	2/2	Labor difficult	2	ND	Periodic depression	Labor difficult	1	ND	Before 6	More prominent split in lower lip	Rainer et al. (128)
2	20	2/3	ND	2	2608	No "neurotic symptoms"	ND	1	2381	Before 4	Phobic and somnambulant as a child;depressed and suicidal later.	Klintworth (82)
3	29	2/2	ND	2	2835	Development normal	ND	1	2835	?(early)	Early stammer; bowel and bladder control later than co-twin	Parker (121)
4	18	1/1	Spontaneous breech	1	1885	Only minor childhood illnesses	Spontaneous vertex	2	1871	?(early)	Gastrointestinal infection neonatally;considered weaker twin	Davison et al. (27)
5	8	ND	ND	ND	Lighter twin	Apparently no serious illnesses	ND	ND	Heavier twin	4	Glandular tbc at 3 years of age lasting 2½ yrs	Green and Stoller (50)
6	20	2/3	Normal	2	3062	Congenital pyloric stenosis;Ramstedt	Normal	1	2977	3-4	More illnesses in childhood than co-twin; later psychosis	Zuger(this report)

ND, no data

Table 2. Birth and Other Factors in Female Monozygotic Twins Discordant for Homosexuality

Case No.	Age First Seen (yr)	Gravid Order	Heterosexual Twin				Homosexual Twin					Reference
			Birth Order	Twin Birth Order	Birth Weight (gm)	Medical and Other Factors	Birth	Twin Birth Order	Birth Weight (gm)	Age Masculine Symptoms Noted (yr)	Medical and Other Factors	
1	ND	2/2	ND	1	ND	Birth mark on forearm and upper lip;schizophrenic	ND	2	ND	ND	Schizophrenic	Rainer et al. (128)
2	39	1/3	ND	2	2722	Menses late and ? scant	ND	1	2722	?(early)	Menses late and scant;slight stammer	Parker (121)
3	24	1/3	ND	ND	?light-er twin	More physical illness than co-twin	ND	ND	?Heavier twin	Before 8	Less physical illness than co-twin	Green and Stoller (50)

ND, no data

Table 3. Possible Familial Environmental Influences on Male Monozygotic Twins Discordant for Homosexuality

Case No.	Heterosexual Twin	Homosexual Twin	Reference

1	Named for father
	Blamed by mother for
	  difficult pregnancy
	"Rejected" by mother
	Hated his parents
		Preferred by mother
		Mother permissive of his
		  homosexual experiences
		Supposed to be weaker
			Rainer et al.
			(*128*)

	Parents wanted boys Both boys discouraged from contact with girls Mother derogated father		
2	Masculine name "Naughty" as a child, more active	Masculine name "Good" child, dependent Mother's favorite (Effeminate boy)	Klintworth (*82*)
	Neither twin reached satisfactory "rapport" with father Both twins preferred mother to father		
3	Masculine name	Masculine name Mother wanted a girl; treat- ed as one from birth on	Parker (*121*)
	Both twins dressed as boys Father remote from both		

4	Masculine name	Masculine name
		Overprotected by mother be-
		  cause of near fatal illness
		Father could not get close
		  to him
		(Effeminate boy)
			Davison et al.
			(*27*)

	Mother dominant, father submissive		

5	Named after father
	More active
		Masculine name
		More cuddly
		Early illness; would not
		  join in activities of co-twin;
		  father "gave up"
		(Effeminate boy)
			Green and Stoller
			(*50*)

6	Masculine name	Masculine name More sickly Would not join co-twin or father in activities A "loner" (Effeminate boy)	Zuger (this report)
	Both closer to mother Father dominant		

Aside from twinning, there is also evidence that factors other than genetic may be operating to produce similar clinical conditions, as in dyslexia, where the type called "developmental," which has significant familial prevalence, may be indistinguishable from the "brain-damaged" type without such familial disposition (*99*).

The paucity in the kind of data thus far considered in the cases from the literature is partly due to the fact that most of the reports seek to explain the discordance in sexual behavior of monozygotic twins wholly or in part by invoking familial environmental influences. These are summarized in Tables 3 and 4.

If the kind of names may be taken as an indication of what the real preferences of the parents were for each of the twins as regards sex, it would not support a differential influence. In five of the six pairs with data, the names were fully congruent with the anatomic sex.

The gender roles provided by the parents with which to identify would seem to be inadequate for many of the twin pairs. This generally seemed to hold true for both twins. But more important is the fact that all the studies reported, except one, were of a retrospective kind. A more contemporaneous and more accurate view of what takes place is made possible by the fact that in the male pairs from the literature, as well as in the pair reported here, the affected twins follow the pattern of the effeminate boy syndrome, a majority of whom later became homosexual. Such boys have been studied prospectively by Green and Money (*49*), Green (*48*), and Zuger (*171*). Direct evidence for this similarity is available in four of the case histories, and it may be inferred from the early onset of its symptoms as holding true for the other two cases.

Table 4. Possible Familial Environmental Influences on Female Monozygotic Twins
Discordant for Homosexuality

Case No.	Heterosexual Twin	Homosexual Twin	Reference
1	Name ? More "handling"	Name derivative of a boy's Less "handling" Mistreated and manhandled by father Rejected by both parents Unwanted pregnancy; attempt to abort Parents favored boys Both twins schizophrenic, but hetero- sexual less affected	Rainer et al. (*128*)
2		Mother dominant Father ill	Parker (*121*)
3	Given girl gifts Given female chores	Given girl gifts Given male chores Parents accepted masculinity	Green and Stoller (*50*)

In the homosexual twin reported here, effeminate symptoms were present as early as 3-4 years of age, though some mothers of cases followed prospectively have noted their occurrence as early as 2 years of age. These may include dressing in women's clothing, using female adornments, expressing a desire to be a girl, preferring to play with girls at their games, gesturing and posturing like a girl, playing with dolls, and showing an aversion for boys' games and sports. In the masculine-oriented girl, the clinical picture is the corresponding opposite of what it is in the boy.

Very early, these children align themselves with their mothers and their interests, and not with those of their fathers, older brothers, or co-twins. They persist in such behavior, at times covertly, in spite of efforts by parents and others to discourage it. On the other hand, such children reject the attempts of their fathers to involve them in their activities. The fathers become frustrated and "give up." (*172*) Even when these children are not sickly, the fact that in the early years they are almost always "loners" evokes the sympathy of their mothers to give them increased attention and to protect them. When seen retrospectively, the sequence of events may look reversed.

The exceptional occurrence of monozygotic twins discordant for homosexuality does not, therefore, detract from the significance of the impressive degree of concordance. But it is possible that factors other than genetic may be operating pre- or paranatally, as they do in other genetically determined conditions. It does not, however, support a familial environmental causation, since the early development of the homosexual twins is like that of single-born effeminate boys with familial environments shown not to be too different from those of non-effeminate boys and where the unfolding of the homosexuality seems to come from the boys themselves.

Summary

This is a report on a pair of monozygotic twins who showed differences in gender role behavior from early childhood, one following an essentially feminine-type pattern and the other a masculine one, one later becoming homosexual and the other heterosexual. This type of development is present in other monozygotic twins discordant for homosexuality reported in the literature, where the pattern of the homosexual child resembles the syndrome of effeminate behavior described for single-born children. In this syndrome, familial environmental factors have been found not to be significant in the development of the homosexuality, and therefore, the discordance in the psychosexual development of monozygotic twins cannot be ascribed to the differential effect of these factors on them. Other possible explanations have been considered.

A Pair of Monozygotic Twins Discordant for Homosexuality: Sex-Dimorphic Behavior and Penile Volume Responses

N. McConaghy, M.D. and A. Blaszczynski, M.A.[1]

In reports of identical twins discordant for homosexuality, the homosexual twins showed the effeminacy syndrome in childhood. This has been considered evidence that the homosexuality comes from the twin himself. The possibility that the heterosexual twin was denying homosexuality has never been excluded. A pair of identical male twins discordant for homosexuality are reported. They showed significant differences in their penile volume responses to moving pictures of male and female nudes indicative of sexual orientations consistent with their statements. The homosexual twin showed the effeminacy syndrome. Aspects of the syndrome can be induced in mammals by altering their hormonal environment during some critical period in their intrauterine development. Discordance for homosexuality in identical twins could be due to one's being exposed to a different hormonal level during such a critical period.

1. Department of Psychiatry, Prince of Wales Hospital, Sydney, Australia.
   Department of Psychiatry, Prince of Wales Hospital, Randwick, 2031 New South Wales, Australia.

ACKNOWLEDGEMENTS

The assistance is gratefully acknowledged of the Blood Bank, Prince of Wales Hospital, and the Red Cross Blood Transfusion, Sydney, in providing the serological and tissue typing results for the twins, and of Dr. E. M. Nicholls, Senior Lecturer, School of Community Medicine, University of New South Wales, in determining the probability that dizygotic twins could show these results.

Introduction

Zuger (*173*) has reviewed English language reports of monozygotic twins discordant for homosexuality. In some of these reports (*82*), it was pointed out that monozygotic twins may differ in genetic structure. However, it was generally assumed that the discordance was produced by differences in the emotional experiences of the subjects, which could plausibly be considered in the light of psychodynamic theories to produce behavioral characteristics of the opposite sex in the homosexual twin (*121,27*). Zuger (*173*) pointed out that in the published studies, whenever the data were given, the homosexual but not the heterosexual male twin showed features of the effeminate boy syndrome (*7,171,6*). Zuger (*173*) described a further pair of male twins discordant for homosexuality in whom the homosexual twin showed effeminate symptoms from the age of 3 or 4 years. He believed that the unfolding of the homosexuality which effeminate boys commonly show at a later age came from the boys themselves, and was not a reaction to their family environment.

Before it can be accepted that the study of monozygotic twins discordant for reported homosexual behavior is relevant to an understanding of the etiology of homosexuality, it is necessary to show that the twins are truly discordant, rather than that both are homosexual, but one has repressed or otherwise denied knowledge of his homosexuality. At least since it was advanced by Freud (*39*) that paranoia could be the result of repressed homosexuality, psychiatrists have been prepared to accept that people can repress, deny, or in other ways be unaware of existing homosexual feelings or impulses. McConaghy (*101*) advanced evidence that, following aversive therapy, significantly more homosexual males experienced reduction or loss of homosexual feelings than did homosexual males who received positive conditioning. Yet members of both groups continued to show comparable penile volume responses to pictures of nude men. This indicates that subjects' penile volume responses to pictures of nude men and women provide evidence of a physiological ability to be sexually aroused by members of one or the other sex, which can be at variance with the subjects' conscious awareness of the degree of such ability. If monozygotic twins are truly discordant for homosexuality and not merely for awareness of homosexuality, they should show significant differences in their penile volume responses to pictures of nude men and women.

The present study reports the penile volume responses of a pair of twins discordant for reported homosexuality, of whom the homosexual twin showed the effeminate boy syndrome.

Subjects

Tom X., the homosexual twin, was referred by his general practitioner because he was distressed by having no heterosexual desires and by being stimulated by the sight of males with well-developed physiques. He had been conscious of this homosexual arousal from the age of 14 years. He was 21 at the time of the interview. He said that he had an identical twin, A. He believed his twin had no homosexual interest and showed normal interest in girls. There were no other siblings. Both twins weighed 60.5 kg. Tom was 183 cm and A. was 185 cm in height. Tom said of his twin, "When I was very young I didn't have an interest in sporty things the way he did. He used to go to football with my father and I didn't. There's an awful lot of things they have in common." Tom believed his father had done everything he could to encourage Tom to share these interests. In the last few years, both he and his brother had taken up golf enthusiastically and often played together.

In answer to specific questioning, Tom said he avoided being hurt more than did his brother. He then repeated that he hated rugby; "I just didn't like hitting the ground." He dreaded physical training because he disliked taking off his shirt because he was so thin. He hated cricket, also. A. enjoyed all these sports. Tom was not called a sissy, but was frequently called unpleasant names by other boys. He said he would just walk away. This did not happen to his brother because he would stand up for himself. Tom said, "I'm a coward at heart." The period when he was aged 8-12 was the unhappiest time of his life because another boy used to pick on him a lot. Tom said, "He would be so nice at times, then suddenly change." Tom said he was closer to his mother than was his brother, but he did not like to do housework. He never wanted to play with girls or to be a girl. He never wore girls' clothes: "I have no interest in girls." Stamp collecting became Tom's major hobby when he reached the age of 8. His brother had no interest in this, but his father did. In the last few years, Tom has read a great deal about astronomy. He reads much more than does his brother.

When initially seen, Tom had told his mother about his homosexual feelings and said he experiences great relief at h: acceptance. He felt he could not tell his brother or father, but, in fact, when seen about a month later, he had done so. They seemed to be equally accepting, and, in the interview with his father, the only negative feeling the father appeared to have was sorrow that Tom "would miss out on so much in life."

The parents provided the following information. Tom was born first and weighed 2.6 kg. A. was born 10 min later and weighed 2.1 kg. They were told by their doctor that the twins shared a common chorion. A. was kept in an incubator 3 weeks. At 1 year, Tom was the larger and stronger twin and was as dominant as A, until the age of 3 or 4.

Both developed asthma around the age of 4, but in Tom it was more severe. At age 5, both twins were admitted to hospital for tonsillectomy, but A. developed complications and had to remain several days longer than Tom. Tom was "always a bit of a worrier about his health." When he swam, he did not like his head to be underwater. He was never aggressive. A. would stand up for himself, but Tom would not. Tom did not like anything physical and did not like being hurt. From about the age of 7, A. led and chose what the twins did. A. was very untidy. His room was a shambles. Tom was very tidy, with everything in its place and books in piles.

Tom was much more fond of animals than A. and had books on birds and wildlife when he was 12. He was more interested in the pet budgerigar and would talk to it. His father said he and A. would talk about sports and he would try unsuccessfully to involve Tom. Both twins were now very interested in and good at playing golf. From the age of 15, A. has become much less shy and more confident than Tom, particularly since A. started work at the age of 17. Tom is attending university full time. Tom is very talkative at home, whereas A. talks very little. Neither twin ever wanted to do housework.

A. did not wish details of his sexual life to be reported, but stated that he was interested in and sexually attracted to girls from about the age of 14 and he had never been aware of any homosexual interest.

Monozygosity of Twins

The parents said that at times they had difficulty telling the twins apart until they reached the age of 6.

They were identical with respect to the eight major blood groups investigated [ABO system, Rh system, Kell (*K*), Duffy (*Fy*), Kidd (*Jk*), *MNSs* system, *P*, and Lewis (*Le*)] and on HLA typing (A and B series antigens). Wilson (*169*), using an American sample population, calculated that the probability of like-sexed twins identical with respect to these eight major blood groups being dizygotic was approximately 3%. The twins reported in this study were born in Scotland, so it can be presumed that Wilson's conclusion would be reasonably accurate in relation to these twins. The probability that dizygotic twins would have the same HLA typing for A and B series antigens is less than one-third (Nicholls, personal communication). Hence, on the basis of these findings, the probability that the twins in the present report are dizygotic can be regarded as approximately 1%.

Table 1. Behavior in Childhood Characteristic of Homosexual as Compared to Heterosexual Monozygotic Male Twin

	Klintworth (1963)	Parker (1964)	Davison et al. (1971)	Zuger (1976)	Friedman et al. (1976)	Present study
Played with girls	+		+		+	
Played with dolls, girls' toys	+			+		
Showed feminine movements, emotions				+	+	
Liked housework					+	
Was envious of girls or wanted to be a girl	+			+	+	+
Spent more time with mother		+		+	+	+
Father less emotionally close	+		+	+	+	
Was called "sissy"			+			
Avoided rough or contact sport	+	+	+	+	+	+
Avoided physical fighting, being hurt					+	
Had lower status with other boys	+			+	+	+
Preferred reading					+	+
Was shy, a "loner"			+	+		+
Was interested in music, acting	+		+	+		
Was neat, tidy, concerned with appearance			+		+	+

Penile Volume Responses

The subjects' penile volume responses were recorded by a method described previously while they were shown thirty 10-sec segments of moving pictures, ten of nude men, ten of nude women, and ten of landscapes. The segments were presented in random order at 1-min intervals.

By use of a pressure transducer, the responses were recorded on a Grass polygraph, and the changes in both subjects' responses were measured from onset to termination of each of the 30 segments.

A. showed penile volume increases to the pictures of women significantly greater than the responses to pictures of men ($U = 99.5$, $p < 0.001$, Mann-Whitney U test). Tom showed mean penile volume increases to pictures of men greater than those to women, but the difference did not reach statistical significance ($U = 38.5$). When A. and Tom's penile responses recorded at the same polygraph sensitivity were compared, A. showed significantly greater responses to pictures of women than did Tom ($U = 6$, $p < 0.001$), Tom showed significantly greater responses to pictures of men than did A. ($U = 5.5$, $p < 0.001$), and there was no significant difference between their responses to landscapes ($U = 33$).

Discussion

The probability that these twins are not monozygotic can be dismissed on the basis of their similarity and the serological and tissue typing results.

The significant difference in their penile volume responses indicated that A. has an exclusive heterosexual orientation, whereas Tom is predominantly homosexual. Ninety percent of men who claimed to be heterosexual or who volunteered for investigation of their sexual responses showed significantly greater penile volume responses to pictures of nude women than to those of nude men, that is, they showed a Mann-Whitney U test score of 77 or more with procedure similar to that used in this study (*100,9*). Less than 10% of homosexual males seeking treatment showed U scores of 77 or above, and over 70% showed U scores of 50 or less.

Bakwin (6) provided the following description of the effeminate boy syndrome. From early life, the boy dresses repeatedly in women's clothes, experiments with cosmetics, and postures and gestures like a female. He avoids boys' toys, games, and rough sports, and prefers to play with dolls. He prefers girls to boys as playmates, but is basically a "loner." He is gentle, helpful about the house, obedient, and neat to an unusual degree. He markedly prefers his mother and often comments admiringly on her clothes and appearance. He shows a precocious interest in art, beautiful materials, and dancing. He often says he wishes to be a dancer or an actor. His attitude to adults is often ingratiating and clinging, and his mother often complains he is bossy.

Behavioral characteristics of the homosexual subjects as compared with their heterosexual monozygotic twin brothers reported in the English literature and in the present study are summarised in Table 1. Blanks in the table indicate that the relevant data were not supplied in studies 1-5. In regard to the present study, 6, blanks indicate features which were not shown by either twin. In no study was the heterosexual twin reported to show any of these behavioral characteristics to a greater extent than the homosexual twin. The similarity of the behavior of the homosexual twin to that of the effeminate boy is apparent. It is also similar to the female sex-dimorphic behavior reported by men with a homosexual component (103).

The fact that avoidance of rough or contact sports was reported to characterize the homosexual twin in all studies suggests that it may be one of the most striking and characteristic sex-dimorphic differences in children. The difference in involvement in rough-and-tumble play also seems the most obvious and most studied sex-dimorphic difference in young mammals. This difference is of particular interest in view of the increasing evidence that it is biologically determined. The evidence suggests that failure of males to show typical rough-and-tumble play in childhood is due to a reduction in amount or efficacy of circulating androgens at a critical period in their intrauterine development (129). Male rats which experience such a reduction in circulating androgens show in adulthood less male copulatory behavior and more female lordotic sexual responses to other males. A similar change in the behavior of adult male rats occurs if, during their prenatal experience, their mothers were exposed to immobilization stress (160). It was suggested that this behavioral change in the male rats was due to their experiencing a reduction, in this case induced by stress, in the output of androgens produced either by them or by their mothers.

As stated earlier, when monozygotic twins were found to be discordant for some behavioral feature or psychiatric syndrome, it was the practice to regard this as evidence that some difference in the psychological environment of the twins was responsible for the discordance. However, monozygotic twins are exposed to intrauterine conditions that can result in marked constitutional differences between them. Campion and Tucker (*20*) stated that 15-30% of monochorial twins suffer from the transfusion syndrome to a greater or lesser degree and that the unique prenatal environment of monozygotic twins has been implicated as a cause of disparities in their intellectual development not found in dizygotic twins. They quote evidence that monozygotic twins have about twice the frequency of congenital malformations as have dizygotic twins and singletons and that they show about 3 times the fetal death rate and a higher infant death rate.

Discordance for homosexuality in monozygotic twins may be due to differences in their psychological environment. In the light of present knowledge, it would seem equally reasonable to consider it due to exposure to different levels of circulating androgens at some critical period in the intrauterine development of the twins. Unequal development of the twins due to such factors as the transfusion syndrome could result in one twin being at this critical period when the other was not. One twin might be stressed differently from the other and, in response, temporarily produce less androgen.

Are There Gay Genes?
Sociobiology and Homosexuality

Michael Ruse, Ph.D.

ABSTRACT. This paper considers recent hypotheses prepared by sociobiologists purportedly giving Darwinian evolutionary explanations of human homosexuality. Four models are considered: balanced superior heterozygote fitness, kin selection, parental manipulation, and homosexuality as a maladaptive side effect of intensive natural selection for superior male heterosexual behavior. The evidence for the models is reviewed, and their philosophical adequacy is considered in some depth. It is argued that although the models pass obvious methodological hurdles and meet other criteria, as yet, the evidence for their applicability is indecisive.

Interest in human sociobiology, the study of human social behavior from a biological viewpoint, continues at a high level. Although the controversy and bitterness sparked by the publication of E.O. Wilson's *Sociobiology: The New Synthesis* (*166*) seems now to be somewhat muted, the ideas and applications of sociobiology receive increasing coverage in learned journals, conferences, and even in the popular press. Indeed, sociobiology was awarded that ultimate American accolade, an expository article in *Playboy* magazine advertised as "Why Modern Science Says You Need to Cheat on Your Wife," or some such nonsense (*114*).[1] Surely the time has come to stop general defenses of or onslaughts on human sociobiology and to start considering in detail

---

1. Actually, once one gets past the title, the article is surprisingly balanced and informative.

specific claims made by the sociobiologists.[2] It is at this level that the real battle must be fought if sociobiology, and particularly human sociobiology, is to prove of lasting value. Following my own prescription, the present paper will consider sociobiologists' various claims and suggestions about an aspect of human behavior that has attracted quite as much interest and controversy in recent years as sociobiology itself: human homosexual inclinations and practices. An exploration of sociobiologists' explanations of human homosexuality will be followed by a critical evaluation of these ideas.

The Hypotheses

Sociobiologists do not have an "official line" on homosexuality, nor at this stage is such a position even to be desired. Instead, the literature contains a number of suggestions and hints proffered with varying degrees of confidence and evidence. Four possible explanations of human homosexuality put forward by sociobiologists will be discussed here, although the reader is warned that at least one of these explanatory hypotheses is at this point so tentative it may be no more than half an explanation. The extent to which any or all of these explanations should be seen as excluding rival explanations is a matter to be left for later discussions.

First Hypothesis: Balanced Superior Heterozygote Fitness

The first of the sociobiological explanations sees human homosexuality as a function of balanced superior heterozygote fitness (Hutchinson (72)). Since this explanation, like those to follow, presupposes some biological background knowledge, a sketch of such background is in order. Readers unfamiliar with biological theory might be well advised to consult Strickberger (*150*). Readers are also directed toward Dobzhansky, Ayala, Stebbins, and Valentine (*30*).

For evolutionary biologists, the crucial unit is the *gene*, which is carried on the chromosomes, passed on from generation to generation, and responsible in some ultimate sense for the physical characteristics of the organism. The gene's random mutation is the raw stuff of evolution.

---

2. Full details of the sociobiology controversy and of general claims made by sociobiologists and their critics can be found in Ruse (*131,132*).

The chromosomes of organisms, including humans, are paired. Each gene, therefore, has a corresponding gene on the other paired chromosome. Such genes are said to occupy the same *locus*; the genes that can occupy the same locus are known as *alleles*. If the alleles at some particular locus are absolutely identical, then, with respect to that locus, the organism is said to be *homozygous* (the organism is a *homozygote*). If the alleles at some particular locus are not absolutely identical, then, with respect to that locus, the organism is said to be *heterozygous (heterozygote)*. An organism might be heterozygous with respect to one locus but homozygous with respect to another.

Organisms pass on to their offspring a copy of one, and only one, allele from each locus. The selected allele is chosen at random. In sexual organisms like humans, therefore, each parent contributes one of the alleles at any locus. This fact about transmission, known as Mendel's first law, can be generalized to groups. When applied to groups it is referred to as the Hardy-Weinberg law, after its co-discoverers. The law can be stated succinctly as follows: In the case of a large, randomly mating group of organisms, if there is no external disturbing influence, and if at some particular locus there are two alleles (A_1 and A_2) in overall proportion $p:q$, then for all succeeding generations, the proportion will remain the same. Moreover, whatever the initial distribution, over the next and all succeeding generations the alleles will be distributed in the ratio: $p^2A_1A_1 : 2pqA_1A_2 : q^2A_2A_2$ (where A_1A_1 is a homozygote for A_1, and so forth).

Now we must introduce the Darwinian element into our discussion of basic biology. Organisms have a tendency to multiply in number – think, for instance, of the millions of eggs that one female herring lays. However, this tendency is necessarily curbed; there is just not sufficient space or food for unlimited growth. The result is the struggle for existence or, more precisely, since passing on characteristics to the next generation is what counts in the evolutionary scheme of things, a struggle for reproduction. The genes must cause physical characteristics that will help their possessors in the struggle; otherwise, the genes' progress through the ages will be halted abruptly, and their organisms will be supplanted by organisms whose genes confer more helpful characteristics. Hence, we get a continual "selection" for organisms with better "adaptations" than others. Such organisms are said to be "fitter," because they are better at reproduction. In the long run, selection for reproductive fitness, when combined with mutation, is what biological evolution is all about.

Although selection normally implies change in gene ratios, with the fitter replacing the less fit, under special circumstances, selection can act to hold gene ratios constant and can even ensure that less fit organisms are maintained in a population. This is where balanced superior heterozygote fitness comes in. Consider a pair of alleles at a locus, and suppose the heterozygote is much fitter than either homozygote. Although the homozygotes might contribute little or nothing to each future generation, homozygotes will keep reappearing simply because, by the Hardy-Weinberg law, some of the offspring of heterozygotes are homozygotes. In certain circumstances, one can get a balance with the same ratios always holding.

Suppose that one has two alleles, A_1 and A_2, in equal ratio and that on the average, each of the heterozygotes produces two offspring, whereas each of the homozygotes produces none (i.e., the population number remains the same). With each generation, therefore, half the genes will be A_1 and half A_2 (because by definition heterozygotes have an equal ratio of genes and thus will contribute an equal ratio). However, by the Hardy-Weinberg law, the new distribution will be: ¼ A_1A_1 : ½ A_1A_2 : ¼ A_2A_2. In other words, as long as the situation continues, 25% of the new population will always be totally unfit A_1A_1s and 25% will be totally unfit A_2A_2s, a situation maintained by natural selection.

The application of this theory to the phenomenon of homosexuality is not that hard to see, but first let us note that balanced superior heterozygote fitness is not merely a theoretical possibility, it does have empirical confirmation. The best known case occurs in the human species. In certain black populations, as many as 5% die in childhood from sickle-cell anemia, a genetic disease. The apparent reason for the persistence of this disease is that heterozygotes for the sickle-cell gene have a natural immunity to malaria, also widespread in these populations. Because the heterozygotes are fitter than either homozygote, the sickle-cell genes stay in the populations, and in each generation, a number of children die from anemia. (For more details, see Ruse (*130*), see also Lewontin (*95*).)

So, what about homosexuality? Two points must be noted. First, although I have been writing of genes causing physical characteristics, orthodox biological theory defines physical characteristics sufficiently broadly to cover all aspects of an organism's makeup, including its behavior and inclinations.[3] Just as the structure of a worker-bee's wings is genetically caused, so is its ability to make a perfectly hexagonal cell. Second, remember that when a biologist talks of an organism being very unfit, this does not necessarily imply that the organism dies before

---

3. As will become clear later, the genes alone do not cause physical characteristics.

reproducing, as does the child affected with sickle-cell anemia. A mule, although it might be tougher than either parent, is regarded as unfit by an evolutionary biologist simply because it cannot reproduce. Despite the example of the mule, however, many, if not most, of the cases of biological unfitness imply or entail unfitness at all levels.

Thus, biological principles dictate to organisms a sort of reproductive imperative. When this is applied to the human organism, conflicts with traditional ethical systems are virtually unavoidable. Quite simply, what we "ought" to do often runs counter to the biologically fittest course of action. Much of our current ethical thinking stems from two major sources: Kantian and utilitarian moral systems. Often, these two influences are mingled, as in the generally accepted belief that we ought to treat human beings as ends in their own right and not simply as means to the achievement of our goals and that we should attempt to maximize happiness and minimize unhappiness for as many people as possible. Clearly, practical application of such belief systems leads to the conclusion that there are times when one ought to limit one's family size. For instance, it is immoral to have 10 children in India (or anywhere else, for that matter).

From a biological viewpoint, however, if one can successfully raise 10 children, this is a much better (i.e., fitter) thing to do than to raise a planned two children. (The claim that society will benefit more from two than from 10 children and that two is therefore fitter than 10 is not pertinent or well taken; remember, biological fitness centers on the individual, not on the group). In other words, what is moral and what is biologically fit are two different notions; the biological unfitness of homosexual persons has no implication for the moral desirability of a heterosexual life-style over that of a homosexual, or vice versa. Indeed, given the present population explosion, it is easy to argue for the moral acceptability of homosexuality.[4]

In light of this, one can think of a possible explanation for human homosexuality. Homosexual individuals are by definition attracted to members of their own sex.[5] Homosexual couplings, of whatever nature, cannot lead to offspring. Hence, someone who is exclusively

---

4. In this paper, I am not arguing for the elimination of homosexuality, neither am I arguing that heterosexual persons ought to become homosexual. Vasectomies are just as efficient a method of birth control as switches in sexual orientation.

5. I am going to rest with a fairly undefined notion of homosexuality: The homosexual individual is attracted to her/his own sex and most probably has sexual relations with her/his own sex. I would appreciate readers' comments on whether I ought to define homosexuality more carefully, and if I should distinguish the different kinds of homosexuality or homosexual men and women.

homosexual cannot have offspring and is therefore effectively sterile, that is, biologically unfit. (Obviously, I exclude here the relatively rare phenomenon of a homosexual person achieving parenthood through artificial insemination.) One might be tempted to conclude that if homosexual men and women fail to reproduce (or reproduce less than their heterosexual counterparts), homosexuality could not possibly be inherited. However, as we have just seen, the mechanism of balanced heterozygote fitness provides a means whereby homosexual genes could be passed on even if homosexual individuals left no offspring at all!

Let us see how this might work. Suppose that homosexuality is a function of the genes and that possession of two "homosexual genes" makes a person homosexual. Let us also suppose, however, that heterozygotes, possessors of one "homosexual gene" and one "heterosexual gene", were fitter than homozygotes for "heterosexual genes"; in other words, that by one means or another, heterozygotes reproduce more than heterosexual-gene homozygotes. It then follows naturally that the existence and persistence of homosexuality is a function of superior heterozygote fitness. Moreover, the theory can easily accommodate the fact that sometimes homosexual persons reproduce. All that is necessary for the theory to work is that they reproduce less than heterosexual individuals. Also note that if one chooses from among the many estimates of the incidence of homosexuality a reasonable figure of about 5% of the total population, this can be accommodated by the theory, for 5% is the approximate figure suggested for sickle-cell anemia. (Needless to say, I draw this analogy not as proof, but simply to show that we are talking about a mechanism which could, in theory, handle the phenomenon of homosexuality.)

Second Hypothesis: Kin Selection

This is undoubtedly the most exciting of the new theoretical ideas of sociobiology, whether applied to animals or humans. It has been shown that, from a biological evolutionary viewpoint, reproduction is the crucial factor, but what precisely does this mean? First, while recognizing that ultimately everything comes back to the genes, it is important to ask what unit of reproduction above the level of the genes is most significant.[6] Until very recently, the majority of scientists, including most biologists, would have argued that in some important sense it is the species, the reproductively isolated interbreeding group, that is the basic unit of evolution. However, without disputing the species' very special position in the evolutionary scheme, scientists are stressing increasingly that the crucial unit of selection is the individual, that is, the reproduction of the individual organism is the cornerstone of evolutionary biology. Even if a characteristic is detrimental to the species, if it is advantageous to the individual in the short run, then selection will preserve it. (See Williams (*164*); Wilson (*166*).)

A second question now arises: Wherein lies the essence of the individual's reproduction? Obviously, it lies in the passing on of the individual's genes, the units of heredity. Note, however, that an individual is not going to pass on its own genes physically. Rather, it is going to pass on copies of its genes. The key fact behind the notion of kin selection is that it really does not matter where these copies come from. What does matter is that an organism be more efficient at perpetuating copies than its fellows.

Remember, however, that organisms are related to other organisms — brothers, sisters, cousins, and so forth — and that by Mendel's law, an organism and its relatives will have identical instances of alleles. Whenever an individual's relative reproduces, copies of the individual's own genes are being perpetuated. In theory, there is no reason why, under certain circumstances, selection should not promote characteristics that make an individual cut down or forego its own reproduction, so long as those same characteristics make the individual "altruistic" toward its relatives — in the sense that the individual increases the relatives' reproductive chances. This is kin selection. (See Barash (*8*); Dawkins (*28*); Hamilton (*53,54*); Wilson (*165*).)

There is actually a little more to the story. With the exception of identical twins, a person is more closely related to her/himself than to anyone else. One has 100% of one's own genes; one's parents, siblings, and off-spring have 50% of one's genes; grandchildren 25%, first cousins 12.5%; and so forth. Hence, under normal circumstances one will prefer the reproduction of oneself even over close relatives.[7] Simple

---

6. I trust that I am not prejudging issues by ignoring the fact that one of human sociobiology's most vocal critics, R.C. Lewontin, has argued (*95*) that the chromosome is more crucial than the gene.

7. Here, as elsewhere, I do not mean to suggest that genetic sociobiological explanations necessarily imply conscious awareness of one's own optimal evolutionary strategy. Often, even with humans, no awareness is presupposed; it is even denied. The point is that the genes program one to behave *as if* one were aware.

arithmetic shows, for instance, that if by foregoing one's own reproduction one thereby increases a sibling's reproduction by over 100%, then it is in one's own reproductive interest to do so, for more copies of one's own genes are thereby transmitted. More generally, if k is the ratio of gain to loss in fitness and if r is the coefficient of relationship of benefiting relatives ($0<r<1$), then for kin selection to work, $k>1/r$ (i.e., if C is cost and B benefit, $C<rB$).

Kin selection is not only exciting theoretically. Its application to the social insects, although still controversial in some respects, is one of the triumphs of sociobiology. The Hymenoptera (wasps, bees, ants) show a distinctive, tight social structure, with hordes of sterile females altruistically raising their mother's (i.e., the queen's) offspring, the males, incidentally, doing no work at all. It is now believed that this is a function of kin selection. (See Oster & Wilson (*118*).)

It is easy to see how an analysis like this would tempt sociobiologists faced with the phenomenon of human homosexuality (Weinrich (*161*); Wilson (*166*)). Assuming that homosexual individuals have fewer offspring then heterosexual individuals, their apparent loss of reproductive fitness could be "exonerated" in terms of the increased fitness of close relatives. All one needs to do is to postulate that homosexual men and women take altruistic or high-prestige jobs such as the priesthood, act as unpaid nannies to the children of siblings, etc. Thus, the siblings (or other relatives) gain in reproductive power and so, indirectly, do the homosexual individuals. If this explanation were true, homosexual humans would be analogous to sterile worker-bees in that they reproduce through relatives rather than directly.

Simple and obvious though this explanatory hypothesis may be, it raises even more simple and obvious queries, not the least being those concerning the imputed altruistic motives and actions.

Third Hypothesis: Parental Manipulation

The key to kin selection is that it does not really matter how one's genes get passed on; what is evolutionarily important is that one increase or at least maintain one's genetic representation in future generations. Parental manipulation presupposes a similar attitude to the workings of natural selection and, likewise, serves to explain human homosexuality in terms of genetically caused altruism. The difference, however, is that whereas the kin-selection explanation regards homosexuality as a form of altruism ultimately of benefit to the nonreproducing homosexual individual, parental manipulation sees homosexuality as a form of altruism which ultimately benefits others, namely, the homosexual individual's parents (Trivers (*156*)). Alexander (*3,4,5*) has most strongly endorsed the general mechanism of parental manipulation, but, as will be shown, he seems to prefer a different primary mechanism for (male) human homosexuality.

Speaking generally and as yet unconcerned with homosexuality specifically, let us first examine the essentials of the supposed mechanism of parental manipulation. Consider an organism with a number of offspring. Clearly, it is in the organism's reproductive self-interest to have its offspring reproduce as efficiently as possible. Although the organism's reproductive interests depend on its offspring as whole, it is not necessarily true that these interests are identical with any one of the offspring taken individually. Indeed, if an organism has more than one offspring, then the parent's interest will not be the same as any individual offspring, for remember that even a parent and its child have only 50% of their genes in common.[8] Consequently, considering a parent organism with a number of offspring, there may be occasions when it is in the parent's reproductive interest to sacrifice one or more of its offspring for the benefits that would accrue to the other offspring. Suppose, for example, that if all the offspring were to pursue their own interests, then only one would survive and in turn reproduce. Suppose also, however, that if one of the offspring were no longer to compete for itself, then as a result, two of its siblings would survive to reproduce. Clearly, this latter situation is not in the interests of the noncompetitive offspring, which is substituting a zero chance of reproductive success for what had been at least a minimally positive chance. (The qualification "under normal circumstances" is required because obviously kin selection might also come into play.)

It would seem, therefore, that if the genes could give rise to behavior in one or both parents that would in some way and under special circumstances cause one offspring to become a nonreproducer, and this were in the parent's reproductive interests, such genes would be preserved and even multiplied by selection. Obviously, the circumstances would have to be rather special. Normally, if a parent would be better off with fewer potentially reproductive children, its best reproductive strategy would be not to have surplus offspring in the first place. However, another way to bring about the same situation would be for the parent's genetically caused behavior to force one offspring not merely not to compete with its siblings, but to aid the siblings in their

8. Obviously, the relationship is no closer if one has only one child; but in that case, kin selection apart, all of one's reproductive hopes rest on that child.

reproductive quest. If the behavior could induce such altruism, it might well pay a parent to have an extra offspring, even though the offspring would never itself reproduce. This, then, is the essence of parental manipulation, although it must be pointed out that, despite the language, sociobiologists do not mean to imply conscious manipulative intent on the part of the parent. Indeed, the mechanism might well be more effective if both parent and child were unaware of what was going on.

The mechanism of parental manipulation has not met with unqualified enthusiasm, even from otherwise committed sociobiologists (see Dawkins (28)). Nevertheless, there seem to be at least some cases in the animal world where parental manipulation actually occurs. The phenomenon of so-called trophic eggs, where, at times of drought or famine, some offspring are fed to others, would seem to qualify as an example.

At this point, and without concerning ourselves too greatly with the question of evidence, let us turn to the more specific question of how parental manipulation might be proposed as a mechanism for human homosexuality. One has merely to suppose that in some way, when it is in a parent's reproductive interests, this parent's behavior could cause a child to switch from developing into an exclusively heterosexual adult to developing into a person with at least some homosexual inclinations and practices. In our era, soaked as we are in Freudian and neo-Freudian speculations, to suppose that a parent can "make a child homosexual" does not require much of a leap of the imagination; to many, it is almost common sense. One must of course assume, as in the case of kin selection, that the homosexual individual is indeed aiding its siblings or close relatives.

According to this view, therefore, homosexual men and women are not born, they are made – by the parents. There are, of course, genetic requirements, too: The parent must have genes that cause homosexuality-producing behavior; the offspring must have genes that permit it to be diverted into a homosexual role.

Fourth Hypothesis: Homosexuality as a By-Product

The fourth and final hypothesis hardly merits the title "explanation"; it is simply an unpublished speculation by one of the leading sociobiologists. However, given the fact that one philosopher of science has responded warmly to the idea and given that it does rather complete a list of the obvious possible ways in which homosexuality could be explained biologically, it seems worthwhile and legitimate briefly to consider the idea. It must be remembered that here we really are in the realm of speculation.[9]

Basically this explanation, credited to Richard Alexander, understands homosexuality (or more particularly, male homosexuality) as a by-product of, or as incidental to, normal heterosexual development. Alexander writes: "It seems to me that an inadequately explored angle, in terms of immediate causes, is the idea that something which selected powerfully for heterosexual success (i.e., reproduction) incidentally renders us all capable of homosexual preference, given particular circumstances especially during development." He goes on to suggest that males compete very intensely for females (more so than females for males) and that just as one of the effects of this competition is that males have higher mortality than females and are more prone to disease and aging – "maladaptive, inevitable concomitants of the higher-stakes, higher-risk male strategy" – so too, "novel or extreme circumstances might be more likely to yield behavior (like homosexuality) that actually prevent (reproductive) success."

Rather than postulating genes directly linked with homosexuality, as was the case in each of the first three hypotheses discussed, Alexander suggests that some feature which ordinarily would enhance an individual's ability to compete in the struggle to reproduce could, in special circumstances, also divert that individual into homosexuality.

Now what could such a feature be? What sort of attribute might usually lead to reproductive success but occasionally sidetrack one into homosexuality? Alexander's candidate is the propensity to masturbate! (Many 19th century sexologists must be happily nodding approval in their graves.) Alexander points out that for most people, and particularly for boys, initial sexual experiences are autosexual: that is to say, boys masturbate a lot. The point here is that, absolutely, boys masturbate a fair amount and, relatively, masturbate more than do girls. Masturbation in adolescence seems normally to be of adaptive significance: one is learning about sex. For boys, however, there lurks the possibility of being switched towards homosexuality. After all, the masturbator is playing with organs of his own sex, and the visual stimuli are much more obvious for males than females. An erect penis, even if

9. This idea comes in a letter written by Richard Alexander (University of Michigan) to Fred Suppe (University of Maryland), February 13, 1978. In a letter to me, Suppe tells me that he thinks the idea has considerable merit.

it is one's own, catches the eye far more than an erect clitoris, especially if it is one's own. Thus the male, as part of normal heterosexual development, treads a fine line between heterosexuality and homosexuality.

> We know that males masturbate more than females (both very likely are concomitants of more intense sexual competition). Moreover, male masturbation provides visual as well as tactual stimuli that are very similar to those involved in some homosexual activities. If one is stimulated sexually a great deal by seeing his own erect penis, then to be sexually stimulated by seeing someone else's is not such a great leap. Even if tactual and other stimuli are not greatly different between the sexes (and they may actually be), the great difference in visual feedback seems to be potentially quite significant.

Does our society have any idiosyncrasies that push males towards homosexuality? Indeed it does, namely, the fact that because so many males must wait so long before they can have heterosexual experiences, their only sexual relief is masturbation. By the time full heterosexual possibilities are available, it may be too late: the masturbating males prefer penises to vaginas. Thus, as a result of changes in society unrelated to sexuality, males are pushed towards homosexuality.

Alexander writes:

> Now, given the above sexual differences, and the likelihood (again, somewhat speculative) of enormous importance of *initial sexual experience*, what's going to happen if society creates a situation in which practically all boys masturbate for years before they have a real heterosexual experience? It seems to me that, for *incidental* reasons, many of them will become predominantly or solely homosexuals, and another large complement may continue to rely on masturbation as a sexual outlet, and may actually teeter on the edge of homosexuality as well. Females would not be so greatly affected.

Concluding this discussion, Alexander suggests that women have more trouble grasping the possible connection between masturbation and homosexuality, presumably because no such connection obtains in women's sexual development.

The Evidence

It is now time to ask: Are any of these four possible sociobiological accounts of homosexuality true? How much evidence is there for or against each of them at present? What new data should be collected in order to test them? Because the sociobiology of homosexuality is so new, many of the pertinent studies remain undone. Empirical science is not a question of simply gathering information, but rather of gathering information in the light of some hypothesis. Until recently, we did not have the sociobiological hypotheses. Now that we do, we can begin empirical studies in earnest, although for the time being we may have to make theoretical bricks with very little empirical straw.

Balanced Superior Heterozygote Fitness

This is still very much a hypothesis and appears to have been proposed for no better reason than because it describes one way to generate less than biologically fit humans. As yet, no study has shown that over a number of generations the ratios and distributions of homosexual to heterosexual offspring match those to be expected were a balanced superior heterozygote fitness mechanism at work. Indeed, it is questionable just how biologically unfit homosexuality actually is. It may be logical to suggest that a man who is attracted to other men will have fewer children than one who is exclusively heterosexual, but many homosexual men have fathered children. How reproductively unfit are homosexual men in our society? How unfit are they in preliterate societies?

Another problem is raised by the existence and nature of women. Fairly central to sociobiological theorizing is the claim that females (excluding fish but including humans) have little command over whether or not they will reproduce (Trivers & Willard (*157*)). Males must compete for females, and hence, many males do not reproduce. Females, however, although they can use certain strategies to get a good mate, tend to be fertilized come what may. Does this imply, as there is empirical evidence to suggest, that lesbians are biologically as fit as their heterosexual sisters? This would not mean that, overall, homosexuality could not be biologically deleterious; the situation would approximate that of a sex-associated characteristic like hemophilia, which appears almost invariably in the male. It would mean, however, that theoretical ratios would change, and one would expect to find empirical evidence thereof.

In short, the balance hypothesis for homosexuality seems little more than a hypothesis, but before abandoning it altogether, one other area of possible evidence should be examined — evidence that may provide some necessary, albeit insufficient, conditions for the truth of the balance hypothesis. I refer to evidence that might be expected to show whether or not homosexuality is a genetic trait (Hull (*71*)).

It is commonly thought (i.e., by nonbiologists) that there is a fairly rigid dichotomy between genetically caused traits or characteristics and environmentally caused traits. Much of the controversy over the causes of intelligence has resulted from the belief that IQ is either a matter of *nature*, something one inherits, or a matter of *nurture*, something one is educated to or otherwise environmentally forced into. As biologists now realize, however, this sharply conceived dichotomy is misleading. All characteristics are in some sense a function of the genes in interaction with the environment. There is virtually nothing that could not be changed by a change in the genes; similarly, there is virtually nothing that could not be changed by a change in the environment. Why am I taller than my father? Partially because my mother's family members are taller than my father's. Partially because (English) children were better fed during the Second World War than they were during the First.

Nevertheless, some characteristics, such as human eye color, are controlled more by the genes in the sense that these characteristics develop on certain pathways, regardless of the normal environmental fluctuations. Conversely, some characteristics, such as speaking English rather than French, are more under the control of the environment in that they are very sensitive to variations in the normal environment, especially during development. If genetic and environmental traits are understood in these qualified senses, it would seem that a presupposition of the balance hypothesis for human homosexuality is that homosexuality falls fairly close to the genetic end of the spectrum. The hypothesis supposes that almost inevitably a homozygote for the homosexual gene will be homosexual and not otherwise.[10]

---

10. Of course, the genes are not themselves homosexual. By "homosexual gene" is meant homosexual-orientation-causing gene.

The question to be asked, therefore, is whether homosexuality is genetic in this sense. Note that a positive finding only provides a necessary condition for the truth of the hypothesis. A characteristic can be essentially genetically controlled in many ways other than through homozygosity for a recessive gene. One could have straightforward dominance of a homosexual gene. Even if it were established that the pertinent causative gene is recessive, this does not prove, as the balance hypothesis claims, that the heterozygote is superior in fitness to all of the homozygotes.

To discover if homosexuality is genetic, one needs to observe situations where one might hope to distinguish genetic from environmental conditions. An experimental situation of growing popularity, particularly with those concerned with the genetics of IQ, is provided by adoption.[11] If one can trace adopted children and their biological and adoptive parents, then one can observe if the children are more like their biological parents, in which case the genes seem to be playing the crucial role, or more like their adoptive parents, in which case the environment seems to be reigning. Unfortunately, in the case of homosexuality, it is not that easy to know to what extent studies of adoption would be applicable. Certainly many homosexual men and women have reproduced; but, as explained earlier, by the very nature of the case the data will be limited because homosexual individuals will tend to be less than fully reproductive. Also, I would imagine that gathering the required information would not be easy. A woman giving up a child for adoption might be prepared to answer questions about the education and jobs of herself and her lover. She might be far less willing to tell all about their sexual inclinations and practices. (Would a pregnant teenager know or admit that her boyfriend was homosexual? Even if she or her boyfriend had had homosexual encounters, how reliable a guide would that be to their adult sexual orientation?)

Much more promising are twin tests. There are two kinds of sets of twins: monozygotic twins, who share the same genotype, and dizygotic twins, who do not and are therefore no more closely related than normal siblings (i.e., 50%). If one finds a significant divergence between the differences between monozygotic twins and the differences between dizygotic twins, then, since generally both twins experience the same environment, a reasonable inference is that genetic factors are involved. There is one major study of this kind, and the results, taken on their own, are astoundingly impressive (Kallmann (75); Heston & Shields

11. I discuss, with references, both conceptual and empirical questions surrounding genetics of IQ in Ruse (132).

(61)). In a study by Kallmann of 85 sets of twins where at least one twin showed homosexual behavior, in all 50 monozygotic cases, both twins were homosexual and, moreover, homosexual to much the same intensity. In the dizygotic cases, on the other hand, most of the twins of homosexual individuals showed little or no homosexual inclination or behavior. One could not ask for stronger evidence of a genetic component to human homosexuality. Indeed, the evidence is so strong one is reminded of Mendel's too perfect figures confirming his pea plant experiments.

Against Kallmann's study it must be noted that since then, cases of monozygotic twins with different sexual orientations have been discovered (e.g., Rainer, Mesnikoff, Kolb, & Carr *(128)*). It certainly does seem that homosexuality has some genetic basis, that it is not exclusively a function of environmental factors. Apart from anything else, it is almost inconceivable that the basic human sex drive, whatever its orientation, would have no genetic causal component. Humans would very soon die out if none of us cared a fig for sex or if we were attracted to cabbages rather than fellow humans. So at a maximum it would seem that, given our genetic sexuality, the environment could establish our preference for members of the same sex or the opposite sex, although no doubt the environment might increase or decrease the strength of our sexuality.

The counterfindings suggest two, not necessarily incompatible, possibilities. The first is that there are multiple causes of homosexuality. Perhaps some forms of homosexuality are essentially a function of the genes, whereas other forms or manifestations require a significant environmental input. Genetically speaking, this is quite plausible. Suppose homosexuality were a function of the number of genes, *i.e.*, if one had more than a certain number, then homosexuality would inevitably appear, but if one had less than that number, then a specific environmental input would be required to cause homosexuality. A person with none of the genes would not be homosexual whatever the input. This is a well-known phenomenon.[12] The second possibility is that at least one form of homosexuality has a genetic base but still requires some kind of special environmental input. Without it, one is heterosexual. (Alternatively, some form or manifestation of heterosexuality might require some kind of special environmental input; without it, one is homosexual.)

---

12. Waddington *(158)* discussed this phenomenon extensively in the context of fruit-fly wing deformities. Whether, as he thought, this is the key to an important evolutionary mechanism is a moot point. (See Williams *(164)*; and also Ruse *(130)*).

It should be added that some of the reported counterexamples to Kallmann's study (i.e., monozygotic twins with different sexual orientations) lend plausibility to one or the other of the above possibilities, both of which require some specific environmental input to produce homosexuality. In the reported cases, there is evidence that within each pair, the twins were treated differently, with the later-to-be-homosexual twin generally getting more mothering, being treated more like a girl (nearly all the cases are of males), and so forth (Rainer et al., (*128*)).

In short, the evidence from twin tests provides fairly strong support for the belief that the genes play some role in homosexuality, although there is also evidence that the environment plays an important role. This brings us full circle back to Freud, for this was precisely his belief (Freud (*38*))! As pointed out, however, this conclusion does not support the balanced superior heterozygote fitness hypothesis as such, although the evidence is certainly compatible with other genetic mechanisms. Moreover, there are findings of another sort which cast doubt on the balance hypothesis. There are statistical findings about birth orders and parental ages at birth of child. In particular, there are significant correlations between male homosexuality and birth order (younger sons have a greater tendency to be homosexual) and between male homosexuality and age of parent at birth (older parents have more homosexual sons). At one point it was thought that the main correlation was between older mothers and homosexual sons, but now it seems that the age of the mother is a function of the age of the father, although indeed mothers are older.[13]

Now, if homosexuality were a simple case of balanced superior heterozygote fitness, these findings should not obtain. There is nothing in normal Mendelian theory, on which the balance hypothesis rests, to account for them. Indeed, an older child would be just as likely to be a homosexual homozygote as would older parents. At the very least, the findings suggest either that there are causes of homosexuality other than a balance mechanism or that the balance mechanism is complicated by other factors, genetic or environmental. At this point, given the lack of positive evidence for the balance mechanism and given the existence of other hypotheses, judicious use of Occam's razor is in order.

One might think that these findings about parental age and so forth would be fatal to any genetic hypothesis about the etiology of

---

13. Abe and Moran (*1*) and Slater (*142*). See also Birtchnell (*14A*), Siegelman (*140*), and Weinrich (*161*). If any readers have any thoughts on this subject, I would appreciate hearing from them.

homosexuality, but this is not necessarily so. First, as has been noted, there might be multiple causes of homosexuality. Some homosexuality could be fairly directly controlled by the genes, and some not so. Although the above correlations point to significant connections between homosexuality, low birth order, and high parental age, they certainly do not deny that some homosexual men and women are first-born or that some have young parents. Second, it is well established that some genetic phenomena are a function of parental age (which is possibly not entirely unconnected with birth order, although not directly causally connected). In particular, the ova and sperm of older people are much more likely than those of younger people to have mutated in certain ways. For instance, older mothers are much more prone to having children afflicted with Down's syndrome (mongolism), caused by an extra chromosome, and older fathers are more prone to children with hemophilia (Hilton, Callahan, Harris, Condliffe, & Berkley (62)). There is, however, no cytological evidence for this hypothesis as it might apply in the case of homosexuality (see Marmor (98)).

Third, and perhaps most likely, the correlations are compatible with a genetic hypothesis if the environment also plays a significant causal role. The correlations suggest a more protective attitude of the parents (particularly the mothers) than is usual and also a child who feels cowed and dominated (and perhaps protected) by older siblings. Furthermore, an older father may play a less active role than usual. It is easy to see how environmental input of this kind could trigger a homosexual orientation in a child who already has the requisite genes. This would also explain why not all younger children or children of older parents are homosexual – most are not! For that matter, we would then have an explanation for why all children of dominant mothers (or whatever the environmental input may be) are not homosexual; they, too, lack the required genes.

I suggest, therefore, that our discussion so far has shown that at least some homosexuality could have a genetic component in the sense explicated above, that it is highly improbable that the environment does not play an important role, that the environmental input might be connected to familial factors such as parental age and birth order, and that while the balance hypothesis has not been proven false, it is unlikely to be the exclusive source of human homosexuality – indeed, its only recommendation is that it is one way to get reduced fertility (which, it is assumed, homosexual individuals have).

Kin Selection

The key equation for the operation of kin selection, it will be remembered, is $C<rB$, where C is the reproductive *cost*, or loss of one's own personal reproductive success; r is one's degree of *relatedness* to the person who benefits; and B is the reproductive *benefit* conferred on the recipient of altruism. Thus, for instance, one's full siblings ($r = 1/2$) must benefit more than twice as much as one loses. There are a number of ways in which this inequality might obtain or be made more likely: if one's personal chances of reproduction are low, if the relationship to the recipient is high, and if the benefits obtained are high.

When applying this theory to homosexuality, it is assumed that homosexual individuals reduce their own reproductive fitness in order to boost the fitness of close relatives, especially siblings. There need not be anything intentional about this, but the effect is that in being homosexual, offspring become altruistic towards close relatives in order thereby to increase their own overall "inclusive fitness." This explanation is genetic in that the homosexual potential exists, but environmental in that the potential requires some reason to be triggered. (Since we are not Hymenoptera, there is no a priori advantage to being homosexual.) In verifying this hypothesis, one would look for some environmental reason suggesting, not necessarily consciously, that heterosexuality would be a bad reproductive strategy. In this, the kin selection hypothesis differs from the balance hypothesis. It differs also in expecting the homosexual individual to be altruistic: Family members must breed better because of a relative's homosexual life-style.

A number of sociobiologists have suggested that a major key to the causes of human homosexuality may lie in this theory of kin selection, and recently James Weinrich has argued the thesis at some length, basing his study on a far more detailed and extensive search of the empirical literature than had ever been undertaken before (Weinrich (*161*)); see also Wilson (*167*)). In line with another position taken by many sociobiologists and described above, Weinrich believes that the most unbiased sources of evidence for possible genetic foundations of human homosexuality lie in "primitive" or preliterate societies, for these most closely approximate early societies when natural selection was having its fullest effects on humans. With respect to homosexuality, Weinrich believes some suggestive extrapolations between preliterate societies and our own are possible.

Now, there are many reports in the anthropological literature of homosexuality of various forms in preliterate societies. One reads of various kinds of cross-dressing involving homosexual intercourse and even, in some societies, of certain forms of homosexual marriage. Unfortunately, because many of the reports concern adulthood almost exclusively, there is little information on whether something had occurred during the childhood of the homosexual adult which would make adult homosexuality an attractive reproductive strategy.

What information there is, however, suggests that adopting a homosexual life-style frequently follows or is accompanied by phenomena that would indeed lower the reproductive cost. For instance, at one time among the Araucans of South America, all ritualized homosexual males "were men who had taken up the role of women, who took 'the passive role' in homosexual relations, and who were chosen for the role in childhood, due to their feminine mannerisms or certain physical deformities" (Weinrich (*161*), p. 170). Among the Nuer, a "woman who married another woman is usually barren" (p. 171). Among the Toradjas, the male homosexual life-style and women's work occurred "primarily because of cowardice or some harrowing experience" (p. 171). Generally, ritualized homosexual roles seem "to be attractive to individuals who have undergone some trauma, regardless of whether this involves a change of sex" (p. 173), although there certainly are exceptions. From a biological point of view, if such individuals have a low expectation of having offspring anyway, they have little to lose by becoming homosexual. In fact, if their siblings have more children as a result, they have much to gain.

Our own society provides some evidence to back up low C (reproductive cost) or low probability of C for homosexual individuals. "In accounts of modern male-to-female transsexuals, it is very common to read of some sort of childhood trauma immediately preceding the appearance of femininity" (Weinrich (*161*), p. 173). A study of a group of effeminate boys (who apparently have a much higher probability of turning out homosexual than do average boys) "showed an above-average incidence of certain physical defects" (p. 173). Two other pieces of information may be pertinent, although Weinrich does not argue from them directly. First, a careful study implied that there are fairly significant physical differences between adult homosexual and adult heterosexual males. On the average (*i.e.*, there are definite exceptions), heterosexual males are heavier, although not taller, by 6.25 kilos and are stronger. As a statistical ensemble, homosexual males "had less subcutaneous fat and smaller muscle/bone development and were longer in proportion to bulk. Their shoulders were narrower in relation to pelvic width, and their muscle strength was less" (Weinrich (*161*), p. 129). Given the fairly strong links between child development and the adult state, one might suppose that as a group, future homosexual males comprise the slighter, weaker children who face the possibility of reduced C, making a homosexual strategy more attractive from a biological viewpoint. (This would be especially true in preliterate societies.) Incidentally, lesbians tend to be taller than heterosexual females; would it make sense to suggest that this reduces their C also? Second, it should be remembered that homosexual children tend to be lower down in birth order. A lower birth order might not be so significant in our own society, but elsewhere this could be a reproductive handicap. By the time the youngest child comes along, most of the family resources, e.g., a family farm, may already have been appropriated, significantly lowering the child's potential reproductive cost. Simply out of reproductive self-interest, it would pay the youngest child not to enter into heterosexual competition. All in all, therefore, it would seem that there is some evidence of lowered C or potential C for homosexual individuals.

At this point, there must be grumblings (or shrieks) of discontent from some readers. "Homosexuals are being presented as sickly, reedy little runts, unable to measure up to their heterosexual siblings! If this is not stereotypic thinking, nothing is." In reply to this objection, two points can be made. First, thanks to modern medicine, in our society, someone who has had a childhood disease can be as perfectly physically fit as an adult. Second, there is nothing vilifying of homosexual men and women in the facts just related. If heterosexual men are indeed heavier and stronger than homosexual men, that is simply a fact. (Before accepting it as a universal truth, however, I would need the evidence of many more empirical studies.) Moreover, if sociobiologists want to seize upon such a fact and use it to explain human sexual orientation, that is their right. After all, homosexuality must have some cause, and in terms of logic, having smaller body weight seems on a par with having a dominant mother, to cite a cause favored by many analysts. Certainly, smaller body weight is just the sort of thing that would attract evolutionists, which is what sociobiologists are, after all. If evolutionists found two races of the same species of animal with significant body-weight differences, they would feel an explanation was in order and would search for other differences and consequences.[14]

---

14. Indeed, the fact that members of different races have different body sizes has been of great interest to evolutionists. It is the basis of the evolutionary rule, Bergmann's principle, that members of races in colder climates tend to be larger than conspecifics in warmer climates. Various explanations have been sought (Ruse (*130*)).

So far we have considered only one side of the equation. The crucial inequality for kin selection is $C < rB$. Although this can be achieved by lowering C, raising B also helps. (I assume we are dealing with a fairly high r.) If a kin selection hypothesis for human homosexuality is to have any plausibility, then we might very reasonably expect to find that B, the amount one can help one's relatives, will be higher than normal. If one persists in linking facts to values, the values here would seem to elevate the status of homosexual men and women.

Again, consulting the example of preliterate societies, Weinrich argues that in such societies, homosexual persons tend to have high status which presumably would redound to the credit of close relatives. Weinrich documents the fact that in society after society, certain individuals adopt the dress and roles of members of the opposite sex, perform tasks appropriate to that sex, and engage in relations with members of their own sex. Moreover, with very few exceptions, homosexual persons have high status within their societies and, because they are considered to have certain special magical or religious powers, they often act as priests or "shamans." Weinrich (*161*, pp. 203-205) catalogues their dignity thus: among the W. Inoits, "advice always followed"; the Araucans, "advice required for every important decision"; the Cheyenne, "goes to war; matchmaker; supervises scalps and scalp ceremonies"; the Illinois, "required for all important decisions"; the Navaho, "wealthy;   leaders,   mediators;   matchmakers;   unusual opportunity for material advancement"; the Sioux, "extraordinary privileges"; the Sea Dyaks, "rich; persons of great consequence; often chief." In short, being homosexual and taking on a homosexual role in such societies often led to very high status and consequent opportunity to advance the cause and comforts of close relatives; that is, homosexual offspring were specially suited to raising the reproductive chances of those who shared their genes, for they could confer a high B on their relatives, which is something else required for the efficient operation of kin selection.

Of course, in our own society it is hardly true to say that homosexual men or women have an elevated status. Indeed, they tend to be despised and persecuted.[15] There does seem to be some evidence,

---

15. A matter on which Weinrich does not speculate is the possible pertinence to his case of a phenomenon in our own society, the Roman Catholic clergy. They have considerable influence, particularly in southern and rural Europe and in South America, and this influence obviously comes from their priestly roles. Is it significant that they abstain from heterosexual relationships and wear clothing which is far closer to that of women than men? It would be interesting to have answers to a number of questions. Does having a priest in the family raise the family's status? Do priests

however, that they have special abilities that would fit well in the roles which they would have been expected to play in preliterate societies where, according to sociobiologists, natural selection would have been having its crucial influence. Indeed, the abilities might even be such as to raise the *B* of homosexual persons in our own society, despite their apparent low status.

For one thing, there is evidence that they tend to have greater acting ability than heterosexual people (Weinrich (*161*), p. 175). Of course, it is notorious in our society that the stage (as do the arts generally) has a far higher proportion of homosexual participants than, say, the teaching profession. It could be that they are attracted to the stage precisely because this is one area where they will be accepted as normal. (Indeed, there are cases of heterosexuals who behave homosexually for the sake of professional advancement within the theater.) There is evidence that homosexuality has an even more complex causal relationship with the dramatic flair. For instance, effeminate boys, a group with proportionately more future homosexual adults than average, "are unusually adept at stage-acting and role-taking – at an age long before they could know that the acting profession has an unusually high incidence of homosexuality" (Weinrich (*161*), p. 175). In other words, there is at least the possibility of a genetic link between homosexuality and acting ability, that is, between some homosexuality and some acting ability. It is obvious that the ability to act would be of value to a priest or shaman, given that so much of their work centers on magic, mysteries, and ceremonies.

The other pertinent piece of information is that homosexual individuals tend to have a higher IQ than their heterosexual peers. Several studies support this claim (Weinrich (*161*), p. 176). Of course, the whole question of intelligence and IQ tests gets one into some very murky areas, and some of the more grandiose and pernicious claims have been very properly criticized. Nevertheless, three pertinent points can be made. First, increasingly there is evidence that intelligence of some form exists and that this shares some kind of causal link with the genes – not, I rush to say, independent of the environment; indeed, this

---

actively aid their siblings and their nephews and nieces? Why do men become priests? Are they often sickly children, are they down the birth order, are their mothers highly instrumental in their career choices? The one question which will probably never be answered is What connection, if any, is there between the priesthood and homosexuality? Was Voltaire's Jesuit the exception or the rule? Of course, one difference between Catholic priests and homosexual shamans is that priests are not supposed to have any sexual relations, homosexual or heterosexual.

kin selection argument rather invokes the environment.[16]   Second, the justifiable criticisms of IQ studies, on the grounds that many are sexually or racially biased, are irrelevant to homosexual studies for which the comparison groups were drawn from similar social, sexual, and racial groups.

Third, and most importantly, the fear that IQ does not really represent some absolute quality of "brightness," but more an ability to get on in society (and to do well on things that teachers value, like IQ tests!) supports the kin selection hypothesis rather than detracts from it. Apparently, almost anyone can raise children, although some do it better than others. What homosexual persons must do, given the kin selection hypothesis, is raise themselves in society to such an extent that they win benefits for their kin, e.g., through influence, find good jobs for nephews and nieces. In other words, homosexual men and women need to possess just those abilities and attitudes that critics fear are reflected on IQ tests. If society demands conformity rather than ingenuity, if the tests measure the former rather than the latter, if homosexual individuals shine on the tests, so much the better for the kin selection hypothesis.

Weinrich suggests that the increased abilities of homosexual people may be the effects of modifier genes. Perhaps a child has a physical injury. This affects its potential C. The child's genes then switch the child towards a homosexual orientation, and modifier genes come into play to increase the child's potential B. It would seem, however, that things could also work the other way, that children with certain superior abilities would be switched towards homosexuality in order that their inclusive fitness might be increased. It is important to emphasize that genes are pretty "ruthless."   The case of the Hymenoptera clearly illustrates that there is nothing biologically sacred about parenthood. If it is in the reproductive interests of an organism to breed vicariously, then so be it. It is biologically possible that in humans, with their newly evolved factor of high intelligence, such reproduction by proxy could be a very attractive option.

How convincing is the evidence for the kin selection hypothesis for human homosexuality?   Although most nonbiologists, and for that matter a good many biologists, find it difficult to take seriously any kind of kin selection hypothesis, I think that our experience with the Hymenoptera shows kin selection to be sensible and a crucial tool in causal understanding of animal sociality. Furthermore, since humans are animals, we ought at least to consider kin selection as working, or as

---

16. I review some of the evidence for this claim in Ruse (*132*).

having worked, on the human genotype. I suggest, therefore, that a case has been made for taking seriously the hypothesis that at least some human homosexuality may be a causal function of the operation of kin selection, if not in our own society, then in the societies of our ancestors.

On the other hand, no definitive case has been made for the hypothesis as yet. For instance, no proof has yet been offered showing that homosexual offspring really do increase the fitness of their relatives and thus, indirectly, increase their own inclusive fitness. Is it indeed the case that siblings of homosexual individuals successfully rear more offspring than they would have otherwise? It would be interesting to know, even in our own society, what attitudes homosexual men and women have towards their siblings and their nephews and nieces. Is there evidence, e.g., in the form of money left in wills, that they help their relatives to reproduce? Similarly, much more work needs to be done on the nature of homosexual people themselves. Do we systematically find that their C or potential C is reduced in childhood? In short, the case seems "not proven." Conversely, it ought to be taken seriously by anyone interested in the etiology of human homosexuality.

Parental Manipulation

In certain respects, this hypothesis overlaps the kin selection hypothesis, and much of the evidence garnered for one applies equally to the other. For instance, if a child has reduced C or potential C, it might be in the interest of the parents, and the child, to direct the child towards homosexuality. Similarly, if the homosexual offspring can and do benefit their relatives, this will help the parents as well as the children. Weinrich's evidence about the causes of shamanism and the status of shamans applies to this hypothesis as well as to the kin selection hypothesis.

The two hypotheses, however, are not identical and can lead to different predictions. What is in the reproductive interests of the parents might not be in the reproductive interests of the child. If a parent has three children and each child raises two children, there will be six grandchildren. Suppose, however, that one child were a nonreproductive altruist, then the others could raise three more children between them. Such altruism would benefit the parent, who would then have seven grandchildren instead of six, but would not benefit the altruist, who would exchange two children for three nephews and nieces, i.e., 2 x 50% of its own genes for 3 x 25% of its own genes. More generally, conflict arises between parent and child over help to siblings, at a C to the child, whenever $C < B < 2C$. Therefore, by identifying cost/benefit ratios, one ought to be able to distinguish between the operation of kin selection and parental manipulation or to recognize the presence of both.

Unfortunately, because we as yet have no quantified statistics on the benefits of having a homosexual sibling, there is presently no direct way to distinguish between kin selection and parental manipulation. What we can do, however, is to ask if there is evidence that parents actively mold or influence their children, consciously or unconsciously, into homosexual life-styles. This must occur if the hypothesis of parental manipulation is to have any truth at all.

In fact, the anthropological evidence is very strong that parents do play such a positive role. In case after case of homosexuality in preliterate societies, as listed by Weinrich (*161*), the parents play a part in encouraging or permitting the child to move towards the status of a member of the opposite sex. For instance, among the Sea Dyaks, in order to take on the cross-gender role of a *manang bali*, "one's father must pay a series of increasing fees to initiate the grown son into the role, and all three investigators (of the phenomenon) agree that the *manang bali* are invariably rich (often chiefs) as a result of their fees for shamanizing" (p. 169). Similarly, in societies where a high bride price is demanded, parents will sometimes shift sons toward a female role, thereby changing an economic liability into an asset.

One might protest that the very opposite is the case in our own society. Most parents recoil from the thought of having a homosexual child. However, apart from the fact that our society may be atypical and inconsequential to long-range evolutionary considerations, it must be remembered that conscious manipulation is not demanded by sociobiology; indeed, control may be more effective if it occurs unrecognized. It is certainly tempting to speculate that when faced with a child who suffers some illness, parents become extraordinarily protective, thus triggering or aiding a switch in future sexual orientation. Again, if there is indeed anything to this whole question of birth order and the age of parents, it is not difficult to see how this might support parental manipulation. As the family gets larger and larger and, coincidentally, as the parents grow older; it becomes more in the parents' interest to raise a child to be altruistic towards the other children, rather than as yet another competitor. So, unwittingly, the mother smothers her youngest with affection, thus turning the child to homosexuality. Conversely, the father may start to lose interest, with the same effect occurring. This, of course, is all very speculative, intended merely to suggest that the parental manipulation hypothesis, like the kin selection hypothesis, deserves further study.

By-Product of Intense Male Heterosexual Competition

This is but a speculative and hitherto unpublished idea, and, as might be expected, it is not yet supported by much hard evidence. How could one test Alexander's suggestion that male homosexuality is a function of intense selection for heterosexual ability gone haywire? Certainly one could test the initial, crucial premise that competition among males is more intense than among females. Moreover, if the premise were true, then by implication there would be significant measurable differences between female homosexuality and male homosexuality — differences that transcend fairly obvious physiological differences, e.g., because males do not have vaginas but do have penises, almost necessarily homosexual males are going to be more anally oriented than lesbians.[17] One could also test whether homosexual males are in some way more aggressive, perhaps more promiscuous, than homosexual females. Of course, Alexander's suggestion does not tackle female homosexuality. One must first invoke some other explanation for lesbianism and then see what the various implications for the possible differences between the female and male homosexualities would be.

The other significant way in which Alexander's suggestion seems to open itself to test rests on the differences one might expect to find between heterosexual and homosexual males. Alexander proposes that homosexuality is somehow a side effect of intense selection for heterosexuality and that masturbation may be a key factor here. At least two hypotheses seem worth checking. First, there seems to be an implication that homosexual males masturbate longer or more frequently or more intensely than do heterosexual males before they have the opportunity of having heterosexual relations. Might one expect to find that if within a certain period after a boy or adolescent starts masturbating he is initiated into heterosexuality, not necessarily actually

---

17. I would especially appreciate comments by readers on this and related points. In skin magazines, one sees pictures of lesbian encounters involving enemas and the like, but presumably, these magazines are directed primarily toward the male market. A survey of homosexual literature designed and read by males and of homosexual literature designed and read by females would be informative here. On this point, the reader might look at Symons (*152*).

going as far as intercourse, he will "turn heterosexual," but if there is no such heterosexual contact, he will "turn homosexual." Of course, how long he masturbates before heterosexual contact will be a function of both the age at which the boy starts masturbating and the age at which he first meets girls as girls. Tests certainly seem possible here, among them: Are homosexual males earlier masturbators than heterosexual counterparts? Do males brought up in the fashion of English public school boys, who live until 18 in an all-male, antifemale environment, really have greater tendencies towards homosexuality?

Second, given Alexander's suggestion, one might expect some physical differences between homosexual and heterosexual males. For instance, one might expect homosexual males to be able to sustain an erection longer and to have bigger penises. This last point may be particularly relevant, especially if one couples it with the claim that human penis size is key in human sexuality. The fact that human males have much larger penises than other primate males might be a factor in sexual attractiveness. After all, because of their upright stance, humans tend to copulate face to face rather than by the male mounting the female from behind. Face to face, the penis is much more visible to the female. It has also been suggested, by Desmond Morris, that the size of the human penis might be a function of the loss of body hair, something else that makes the penis more obvious (see Wilson (*166*), p. 554). Since the crux of Alexander's suggestion is that homosexuality is a function of adolescent masturbation, it is easy to see how having a somewhat larger penis might lead to an increased "penis fixation." One might think that if very large penises were causing homosexuality, natural selection would quickly step in to control the situation. Recall, however, that in Alexander's hypothesis, the crucial factor must be something which normally helps the individual in the reproductive struggle. It is the "super male" frustrated by lack of heterosexual outlets who seeks satisfaction elsewhere.

It would be very interesting to know how significant a factor penis size really is in sexual attraction. Western males seem to think that a large penis is a desirable attribute. Many Western females must have picked up similar ideas, if only because magazines like *Playgirl*, aimed at women but produced by men, emphasize features prized by men. This, of course, has been going on for some time. Think of *Fanny Hill*, written by a man, where the women remain unmoved by anything less than a maypole. Are women really aroused by large penises, or, more pertinently, are women in preliterate societies aroused by large penises? Where does this particular attribute stand on a list of sexually attractive features?

Another fruitful area of inquiry concerns the question of whether delay of heterosexual relations leads to homosexuality. I know of no firm evidence that it does. Being cut off from heterosexual relations in one's adolescence can lead to homosexual practices when one is an adolescent – English public schools attest to the fact. Whether prolonged autosexuality causes homosexuality is another matter. However, does the denial of heterosexuality, and perhaps the indulgence in homosexuality, during adolescence really increase the chances of adult homosexuality? Do societies that bar adolescent heterosexuality, and perhaps also adolescent homosexuality, produce a higher proportion of homosexual adults than societies that allow or perhaps encourage adolescent heterosexuality? In short, all one can say is that Alexander's suggestion deserves investigation, but that at this point, it remains only a suggestion.[18]

Biological Science, Social Science, and Homosexuality

By this point, my own feelings about the present state of the science must be fairly obvious. I think that the sociobiology of homosexuality is a viable source for scientific hypotheses and well worth investigation; I believe that all who concern themselves with the etiology of homosexuality ought to take sociobiology seriously. As yet, however, the sociobiology of homosexuality lies more in the realm of the hypothetical than the proven.[19] That the genes do play some role in homosexuality seems to be almost certain, that the environment plays some role in homosexuality seems just as certain, but we are still a long way from sorting out the respective components.

What more needs to be said? Perhaps a few words of comfort and encouragement to the social scientists. Social scientists tend to be horrified of and hostile towards biological science. Insecure at the best

---

18. Evidence from studies by the Kinsey Institute suggests that male homosexuality is more common than lesbianism, having a 3-1 bias, and also that homosexual males tend to be far more promiscuous than lesbians. Both of these facts add to the plausibility of Alexander's hypothesis, but one could really evaluate their full significance only if one had some likely hypothesis about the causes of lesbianism. In many ways, a detailed study of the differences between homosexual females and males would be most valuable in the search for causes.
19. As a race, modern philosophers, as most people in the arts, tend to fear and be hostile towards science. It will therefore come as no surprise that eminent philosophers have already started pontificating on the conceptual impossibility of human sociobiology (e.g. Hampshire (55)).

of times, they spend troubled nights dreaming of the bogey "reductionism," the rape of the social sciences as biologists move into the human domain. Of course, social scientists are not alone in their fear of reductionism. Those same, very arrogant biologists have much the same fears when faced with the physical sciences; "every biologist suffers from physics envy." In fact, social scientists may take comfort from what has happened to biology as a result of the reductionist impact of physics and chemistry.   Although in the 1950s, eminent biologists feared that molecular biology spelled their redundancy, precisely because of the coming of the physical sciences, biology flourishes today as never before. Molecular concepts and techniques have opened up whole new areas of discovery and theory in the biological world.   As so often happens, the would-be conquerors have been assimilated to the mutual benefit of all.

What about the interaction between the biological and the social sciences? Can we expect to see the same kind of fruitful interaction and melding? My own feeling is that we can and that the sociobiology of homosexuality illustrates this point perfectly.   Modern genetic thinking – specifically, genetic thinking about homosexuality – emphasizes that it is not the genes alone that cause physical characteristics, including social behavioral characteristics.   Rather, the genes *in conjunction with the environment* cause these characteristics.   I believe the second half of this conjunct, the environment, leaves full scope for the legitimate and fruitful working of social science.

Let me illustrate my argument by reference to the causes of homosexuality.   At this point, I am not particularly concerned about the absolute truth of the explanations I shall be considering: I use them to make a theoretical point.   Doubtless, what I have to say will be generalizable to other situations and to other putative explanations that still await convincing confirmation.

Probably the most famous of all theories of homosexuality is the Freudian explanation for male homosexuality.   All young boys are in love with their mothers.   If they are to mature into heterosexual adults, at some point in their psychosexual growth they must learn to transfer this love to other females.   Some boys, however, find it impossible to break from their mothers; the emotional links are too strong.   This may well be a function of the mother being overinvolved and the father being withdrawn or hostile.   These boys sense that there is something wrong with this situation: They are caught in an incestuous relationship, and humans have a universal horror of and aversion to incest.   Unable to break from their mothers, they transfer their feelings of distaste for an incestuous relationship with a female to the rest of the female sex.   Such boys, and when grown, such men, are unable to respond sexually to females and, consequently, direct their sexual affections and behaviors to males. Significantly, homosexual males usually retain a very close bond with their mothers and often have very friendly nonsexual relations with other women, inasmuch as they can be seen as mother figures. The Freudian explanation is drawn from the social sciences. Now consider an explanation drawn entirely from the biological sciences, namely, the sociobiological explanation of homosexual behavior as the result of parental manipulation (where, remember, this need not be conscious manipulation). Are the two explanations rivals, in the sense that one excludes the other? No, rather they complement each other. The biological explanation sets certain parameters and limits, indicating gaps which can then be filled by the psychoanalytic explanation. The biological explanation does not, however, uniquely demand the psychoanalytic explanation. The biological explanation says that parents manipulate their offspring into homosexuality. The psychoanalytic explanation tells how this manipulation takes place, namely, through mothers being overprotective and fathers withdrawn.

Without suggesting a unique relationship between the parental manipulation hypothesis and the Freudian story, and without presupposing the absolute truth of either explanatory account, I would add that the putative facts about parental ages and birth orders of homosexual offspring are highly suggestive. If, indeed, the parents are older and homosexual children tend to be somewhat low on the birth order, as pointed out above, this would fit in well with a parental manipulation explanation. As the parents' family grows, and coincidentally, the parents grow older, their reproductive strategy may favor an altruistic homosexual offspring over a competing heterosexual child. It is easy to imagine the form their manipulation might take: The father becoming indifferent and the mother becoming overprotective, just what the Freudian account supposes. It is worth emphasizing again that none of this need occur at the level of consciousness.

I suggest, therefore, that social scientists need not fear the coming of sociobiology. Specifically, conventional sexologists need not fear the sociobiology of homosexuality. Rather, the two disciplines can interact fruitfully. This being so, perhaps one final comment of a more philosophical nature may be permitted. Philosophers analyzing scientific change have tended to see it as falling into one of two camps. When a new theory comes along, some believe that the new theory *replaces* the existing theory, in the sense that the new theory proves the old theory wrong. Alternatively, some believe that a new theory absorbs the older theory or *reduces* it to a deductive consequence of the more general newer theory (Hull (*70*); Ruse (*132*)).

I suggest that in the interaction between the biological and social sciences, we should look more for a process of reduction than replacement, at least as regards the explanation of human sexuality. Nevertheless, and this may mitigate the grumblings by social scientists that they no more want their work to be called the deductive consequences of biology than to be replaced by it, I would argue that the prospective absorption of social science would be something at once weaker and less threatening than straight deduction. Consider, for a moment, the way in which parental manipulation is supposed to work. As can be seen, although a place is created for the operation of parental manipulation, its exact nature is left blank. One cannot deduce how this parental manipulation will work. In the case of homosexuality, for instance, mothers could just as easily be hostile as loving. In short, rather than the deduction of the theories of social science, what we have is a need for social science to complement biological science and to explain what is going on at the phenotypic level about which the biology is silent. I do not imply that biology is always silent about the phenotypic level, far from it. I mean, rather, that in the human social context, biologists are as yet ignorant of much of the workings at the phenotypic level. Social scientists have worked at this level and, consequently, are already far ahead in a field that biologists would otherwise need to explore all by themselves.

I conclude, therefore, that the causes of homosexuality point to a more subtle relationship between the biological and social sciences than conventional philosophy might lead one to expect. More importantly, the future for both areas of scientific inquiry looks exciting and stimulating as they now begin to work together.

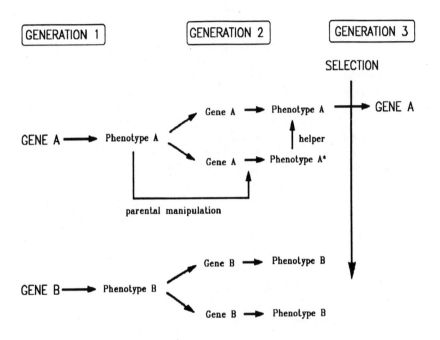

Homosexuality in
Monozygotic Twins
Reared Apart

Elke D. Eckert, Thomas J. Bouchard, Joseph Bohlen, and Leonard L. Heston[1]

We describe six pairs of monozygotic twins, in which at least one member of five pairs were homosexual, and one of the remaining pair was bisexual, from a series of 55 pairs, reared apart from infancy; all the female pairs were discordant for homosexual behavior. This and other evidence suggest that female homosexuality may be an acquired trait. One male pair was concordant for homosexuality, while the other was not clearly concordant or discordant: this suggests that male homosexuality may be associated with a complex interaction, in which genes play some part.

There have been a few reports of homosexuality in male twins ascertained as part of a series. Kallmann (75) reported 100% concordance in 37 monozygotic (MZ) pairs, compared to 12% in 26 dizygotic (DZ) pairs, but came to regard that rate for MZ pairs as excessive, because the twins were recruited from the "clandestine world" of New York City homosexuals of the 1940s, which might favor over-inclusion of concordant pairs. In a series of 14 MZ pairs ascertained

1. Elke D. Eckert, M.D. *Associate Professor of Psychiatry, University of Minnesota,*
   Thomas J. Bouchard, M.D., *Professor of Psychology, University of Minnesota,*
   Joseph Bohlen, M.D., Ph. D., *Psychiatric Resident at Southern Illinois University School of Medicine,*
   *Leonard L. Heston, M.D., *Professor of Psychiatry, University of Minnesota, Box 393, Mayo Building, Minneapolis, Minnesota, 55455, U.S.A.*

*Correspondence

because of criminality, Lange (*93*) found homosexuals in one concordant and one discordant pair.   Sanders (*134*) located twins through homosexual probands, and found five of six MZ pairs concordant.   Habel (*52*) started with five MZ and five DZ probands in German prisons; he found three of the MZ and none of the DZ co-twins to be homosexual.   In an unselected series of 495 German twins, Koch (*83*) found one pair of discordant DZ males, and one pair of discordant MZ females.   Heston & Shields (*61*) obtained proband twins from consecutive admissions to London psychiatric facilities.   They described five MZ pairs, two definitely concordant, two definitely discordant, and one equivocal: among seven DZ pairs, one was concordant.   In addition, they described a family with 14 siblings, including three sets of male MZ twins: all of the twin pairs were concordant − two for homosexuality, and one for heterosexuality.   A family in which six out of ten siblings were homosexual was later described by Dank (*24*).   However, we know of no systematic studies of sexual orientation based on a series of twins, which included either female twins, or twins reared apart.

The use of twins to estimate the relative contribution of genetic and environmental factors to phenotypic traits is well known, and authoritative reviews are available (*69,46*).   Only one special problem of analysis will be discussed here − the search for specific environmental factors which might reasonably be associated with specific phenotypic dissimilarities between members of an MZ pair.   Such dissimilarities, which are evident in all pairs examined, must be non-genetic, and should in principle, be traceable to environment.   In typical studies, the heritability of behavioral traits has been estimated at about 0.5, leaving sufficient scope for environmental effects (*17*).   Yet assiduous searches, albeit mainly retrospective, for specific environments which affected only one member of a pair, and which therefore might underlie discordance, have yielded few findings (*69,123*).   In large part, this failure might be due to the special environments of twins reared together, which include the presence of a genetically identical individual. They may be so similar for each member of a pair that differences in environment possibly associated with phenotypic differences may be too fine to be caught in the crude nets provided by our instruments for assessing environments.

The study of twins reared apart from infancy removes the confounding effects of environmental similarity.   Thus similar outcomes for MZ pairs reared apart may be more confidently associated with shared genes, and dissimilar outcomes may be more clearly associated with environmental factors, because the early environments are more likely to be definably different. Further, one major confounding environmental factor will be eliminated – the other identical twin.

Method

At the University of Minnesota, we have recruited twin pairs who had been reared apart, and have brought them to Minneapolis for a week of intensive psychological and medical study. The procedure included standardized medical-psychiatric interviews and examinations, and questionnaires and interviews concerning current and past sexual practices. Zygosity was established through blood typing. A complete description of the recruiting and study methods was given by Bouchard *et al.* (18) Among the 55 pairs so far studied (counting two sets of triplets as three pairs each), members of five MZ pairs, two male and three female, described themselves as homosexual. A member of a sixth pair of MZ females has extensive homosexual experience, and is regarded as bisexual. The twin who first became known to our group was the homosexual member of a female pair in one case. In the other three female pairs, both members were approached at the same time, and were persuaded to participate in the study by one of the investigators (TJB); both members of the concordant male pair agreed to participate after discussion with their parents. In the other male pair, contact was first made with the twin who regarded himself as exclusively heterosexual; these twins agreed between themselves to participate. The exclusively homosexual twin volunteered information about his homosexuality in his first telephone contact with one of the investigators (TJB). None of the 16 DZ pairs included a homosexual.

That the twins are highly selected cannot be doubted; they are not representative of twins or homosexuals. Nevertheless, study of them has yielded clues which warrant description. In the following descriptions, details have been changed in order to protect the twins' identities.

Table I
Clinical details of male pairs

Twin 1a

Examination

Age 25, weight 58.3 kg, height 180 cm.

Development

1st born, weight 2.67 kg, height 49.5 cm. Pubic hair, age 12; facial hair, age 14; masturbation, age 13; first aware of his homosexuality, age 13; limited heterosexual petting, age 14; no heterosexual dating.

Sex practice

No heterosexual intercourse; homosexual experience starting age 13. Less active sexually than twin; estimates he has had homosexual contact with 25-30 men. Homosexual partner to twin, age 24.

Other

Learning disability, hyperactive, speech impediment with lisp as child. Emotionally labile, subject to episodes of anxiety and depression.

Twin 1b

Examination

Age 25, weight 59.8 kg, height 175 cm.

Development

Second born, weight 2.56 kg, height 49.5 cm. Pubic hair, age 12; facial hair, age 14; masturbation, age 12; some heterosexual petting and dating starting in late teens.

Sex practice

Several heterosexual contacts with intercourse starting age 19; homosexual experiences starting age 13. More sexually active than twin, estimates he had had contact with about 500 men. Homosexual partner to twin, age 24.

Other

Learning disability, hyperactive, speech impediment with lisp as a child. Emotionally labile and subject to episodes of anxiety and depression. Hospitalized three times for depression, anxiety, and anger outbursts.

Twin 2a

Examination
Age 35, weight 71.0 kg, height 175 cm.

Development
Birth order, wt, ht, unknown (but said to be larger than twin at birth). Pubic hair, age 14; facial hair, age 17; masturbation, age 13. Some heterosexual dating in high school, but no sexual contact.

Sex practice
First homosexual contact age 12. Two brief heterosexual contacts age 17-18. Regarded himself as bisexual until age 19 when he became exclusively homosexual. Has had homosexual contact with seven men; prolonged contact with one man. Feels sexually attracted to twin, but no sexual contact with him.

Other
Enuretic until his teens. Adopted into large family on East coast.

Twin 2b

Examination
Age 35, weight 76.2 kg, height 173.5 cm.

Development
Birth order, ht, unknown, weight 1.9 kg. Pubic hair, age 15; facial hair, age 15; masturbation, age 15; some heterosexual dating and petting in high school.

Sexual practice
Homosexual affair with an older man between ages 15-18. First heterosexual experience, age 20, with future spouse. No heterosexual contact, except with spouse. Married age 20, four children. Regards himself as exclusively heterosexual. Sexual relations once or twice a month. Happy with his sexual adjustment.

Other

Adopted and raised by a family in a small Southern farming community.

Results

The male pairs

A male pair, seen by us shortly after their reunion at age 25, was the result of a normal pregnancy. After an unremarkable postnatal course, they were adopted by different families of similar middle-class status, who lived in different suburbs of a major western city. Neither twin knew that the other existed until one went into a bar frequented by homosexuals in a neighboring city, and there was mistakenly identified as his brother. Their histories were strikingly similar. As children, both had been hyperactive, had learning disabilities, and had speech impediments, mainly lisps. Both were emotionally labile and subject to episodes of anxiety and depression. Both had been active homosexuals since age 13, starting with boys in their neighborhoods. Although the second-born boy had had a few heterosexual contacts, both had been aware of being intensely attracted to males and indifferent to females since late childhood. After discovering each other, they became sexual partners.

The second pair, tested four years after their reunion at age 35, was also the product of a normal pregnancy and delivery. One twin weighed 1.9 kg; his co-twin was said to be larger at birth and was 2 cm taller as an adult. The larger twin was adopted by a family living in a large city on the U.S. East coast. He had homosexual relationships starting about age 12; at age 17-18, he had two brief heterosexual contacts which led him to regard himself as bisexual until age 19, when he became exclusively homosexual. He felt sexually attracted to his co-twin, who had been adopted and reared by a family living in a small Southern farming community. He had married, had four children, and regarded himself as exclusively heterosexual. However, between ages 15-18, he had had a homosexual affair with an older man who lived in the same town. His only female partner has been his wife and, although intercourse is infrequent, he described his current sexual adjustment as a happy one. Table I contains further details.

The female pairs

Table II presents the major features of the four female pairs. Without reservation, three of the four pairs were discordant for sexual preference. One member of pair 4 had had a homosexual affair, which was intense and prolonged, so that we regard her as bisexual, although she describes herself as exclusively heterosexual since her second marriage in her late twenties. Her co-twin, like the other three co-twins, denied any homosexual experiences, and described herself as enthusiastically heterosexual.

All four pairs were adopted by normal families which did not have especially notable features. All were reared in medium-sized cities or suburbs, except for twin 2b, who was reared in a small town that was exceptional for its geographical and cultural isolation. In every pair, the homosexual member was the larger throughout life, but had experienced menarche later than her co-twin. The homosexual twin also lagged behind her co-twin in the development of secondary sex characteristics and in the age at which sexual experiences commenced. After menarche, the menstrual history of the two pairs for whom adequate information was available did not distinguish the homosexual from the heterosexual twin.

Table II
Clinical details of female pairs

Twin 1a

Examination

Age 35, weight 63.2 kg, height 164 cm.

Development

Birth order, wt, ht, unknown; tomboy before puberty; menarche age 12-13; breast budding, age 10; masturbation, age 10; limited heterosexual petting, age 16; but no dating.

Sex practice

Age 19 had heterosexual intercourse, not pleasurable, and during same year, realized that she was homosexual. First orgasm, mid 20's. Has had affairs with five women, the last and current eight years in duration.

Other

Enuretic to age 12, probable addiction to sedative drugs age
25.

Twin 1b
Examination
Age 35, weight 62.2 kg, height 158 cm.
Development
Birth order, wt, ht, unknown; menarche age 10.5; breast
budding, age 8; masturbation, age 11; heterosexual dating
and petting in teens.
Sex practice
Age 18, heterosexual intercourse. Age 25, only marriage,
which has continued to date. No homosexual experience.
Heterosexual intercourse two to three times weekly, enjoyed.

Twin 2a
Examination
Age 40, weight 82.1 kg, height 163 cm.
Development
Birth order, first; birth wt, 3.38 kg; menarche age 14; breast
budding and pubic hair, age 13; masturbation, age 13.
Sex practice
Age 16 had heterosexual intercourse, then with several men
through age 18; 'could take it or leave it'...'boring'; one
induced abortion. By 18, knew self to be homosexual and
has had affairs with several females.
Other
Alcohol problem in past – described loss of control drinking;
also amphetamine abuse. Major depression after suicide of
female lover.

Twin 2b
Examination
Age 40, weight 65.6 kg, height 160 cm.
Development
Second born; birth wt 2.0 kg; menarche age 11.0; breast
budding and pubic hair, age 11; 'tomboy' before puberty;
dating age 18; no masturbation.

Sex practice
First intercourse age 18, exclusively heterosexual. Marriage age 22, three children. Describes current sex as 'somewhat unimportant.'

Other
Reared in small, geographically isolated community which, together with strict religious practice in home, limited opportunity for early dating. Age 16 suspended from school for fighting.

Twin 3a

Examination
Age 35, weight 55.6 kg, height 163 cm.

Development
Second born; weight 3.0 kg and length 45.25 cm. Menarche at age 13; age 10 breast budding and pubic hair; masturbation age 17; heterosexual dating through last one to two years of high school (age 17+); age 20, first heterosexual intercourse. Through age 24 to 25, heterosexual contact with about 12 males; never married or engaged. Age 27, first homosexual affair − 'knew' she was homosexual.

Sex practice
Living with female sexual partner since age 28 toward whom she expresses deep emotional attachment.

Twin 3b

Examination
Age 35, weight 53.5 kg, height 162 cm.

Development
First born, 2.7 kg, 42 cm. Menarche age 11; pubic hair age 11; breast budding age 12; dated age 15; first intercourse age 17; married age 18, four children. No homosexual contacts or feelings.

Sex practice
'Very satisfied' with sex life in marriage.

Twin 4a

Examination

Age 48, 79.5 kg, 165 cm.

Development

First born; menarche age 10.3; breast budding and pubic hair age 9. No dating until age 21; heterosexual intercourse age 22; age 23, first marriage from which one child. Age 25, first homosexual contact, then three years with two successive female partners. Age 29, second heterosexual marriage, which has lasted to date with no homosexual contacts; second child.

Sex practice

Since age 29 regards herself as exclusively heterosexual with good heterosexual marriage and active sex life. At same time, feels sexually attracted to both males and females.

Twin 4b

Examination

Age 48; 92.5 kg, 164 cm.

Development

As child of 7, vagina was penetrated by adoptive brother, who was then age 9; menarche age 9.5; breast budding and pubic hair age 8; heterosexual intercourse, age 12; child at age 14; first orgasm and marriage age 16. Divorced and remarried age 35.

Sex practice

Active heterosexual sex life, never homosexual contact. Was prostitute for one year between marriages.

Other

Significant depression after divorce.

Discussion

The male pairs are typical of others which have been described, with the single main difference that they were reared apart in different environments. One pair was clearly concordant for homosexuality. Whether to count the other pair concordant or discordant, or partially one or the other, is problematic; analogous problems of classification often occur in twin studies. It is notable that the male homosexuals said that they were attracted sexually by their co-twins. Twins reared together strongly deny such feelings according to Kallmann's experience, and ours (*61*), although exceptions have been reported (*115*).

Overall, the male pairs tend to confirm earlier studies of twins and twin families: the concordance rate for sexual orientation among MZ pairs is consistently above that of DZ pairs, and despite all problems of ascertainment and diagnosis, it is hard to deny genetic factors an etiological role.

The female pairs yield evidence leading in an opposite direction. Either three or all four of our female pairs were discordant, depending on how one classifies twin 4a. This evidence suggests that in the women, environmental factors were decisive. Moreover, in each pair, the homosexual twin was taller and heavier, but achieved menarche later. In our four pairs, the mean difference in age at menarche was two years, whereas in a normative series, the mean difference is about 0.3 year (*37,149,42*). In our series, the 15 heterosexual female MZ pairs averaged 0.9 years difference in age at menarche, or 1.1 years less than the homosexual twins. In the homosexual pairs, the interval between the menarche of the first and the second twin, was significantly greater than the comparable interval observed in either the normative series, or in our reared-apart heterosexual twins (*P*<0.05, Mann-Whitney U statistic).

The difference of 0.6 years between members of our heterosexual pairs and normative pairs may well be associated with the separate rearing of our pairs. Shared rearing environments, or a tendency for twins reared together to compare notes when asked about developmental milestones, could logically explain the small difference in reported age at menarche between our heterosexual reared-apart twins and reared-together twins.

This pattern of findings suggests that female homosexuality is a trait acquired after conception, most likely after birth, but before menarche. It may be associated with delayed puberty and just possibly with larger physique. With this possibility in mind, we reviewed the medical history of our twins, but found no episodes of illness or other events which differentially affected the homosexuals.

These findings are descriptive only, and should be regarded as clues upon which to base hypotheses; *e.g.* do lesbian women tend to have menarche at later ages than do their heterosexual female siblings? If so, this would support our findings, and it would seem to warrant search for an acquired cause, perhaps an endocrinopathy. Neuroendocrine differences may be associated with male homosexuality *(43)*. Our evidence, though based on a small sample, implicates environmental factors as the major determinant of female homosexuality. If this remains a constant finding, it will, apart from general features of a culture such as language, be the strongest evidence known to us which attributes a major behavioral complex exclusively to environmental factors.

Combined Bibliography

1. Abe, K., and Moran, P.A.P.: "Parental Age of Homosexuals," *British Journal of Psychiatry*, v. 115, p. 313 (1969).
2. Alexander, F.: *Fundamentals of Psychoanalysis* (New York, 1942).
3. Alexander, R.D.: "The Search for an Evolutionary Philosophy," *Proceedings of the Royal Society of Victoria Australia*, v. 84, p. 99 (1971).
4. --------: "The Evolution of Social Behavior," *Annual Review of Ecology and Systematics*, v. 5, p. 325 (1974).
5. --------: "The Search for a General Theory of Behavior," *Behavioral Science*, v. 20, p. 77 (1975).
6. Bakwin, H.: "Deviant Gender-Role Behavior in Children: Relation to Homosexuality," *Pediatrics*, v. 41, p. 620 (1968).
7. --------, and Bakwin, R.M.: "Homosexual Behavior in Children," *J Pediatr*, v. 43, p. 108 (1953).
8. Barash, D.P.: *Sociobiology and Behavior* (New York, 1977).
9. Barr, R.F., and McConaghy, N.: "Penile Volume Responses to Appetitive and Aversive Stimuli in Relation to Sexual Orientation and Conditioning Performance," *British Journal of Psychiatry*, v. 119, p. 377 (1971).
10. Bauer, J.: *Constitution and Disease* (New York, 1942).
11. Bell, A.P., Weinberg, M. and Hammersmith, S.: *Sexual Preference*, esp. p. 216 (Bloomington, 1981).
12. Bene, E.: "On the Genesis of Male Homosexuality: An Attempt at Clarifying the Role of the Parents," *British Journal of Psychiatry*, v. 111, p. 803 (1965).
13. Benedek, T.: "The Functions of the Sexual Apparatus and Their Disturbances," in Alexander, F.: *Psychosomatic Medicine* (New York, 1950).
14. Bieber, J., *et al.*: *Homosexuality* (New York, 1962).
14A. Birtchnell, J.: "Birth Order and Mental Illness: A Control Study," *Social Psychiatry*, v. 7, p. 167 (1972).

15. Boklage, C.E.: "Embryonic Determination of Brain Programming Asymmetry," presented before the First International Congress of Twin Studies, Rome, October 1974, in press at that time.
16. Boss, M.: *Meaning and Content of Sexual Perversions* (New York, 1949).
17. Bouchard, T.J.: "Twins Reared Together and Apart: What They Tell Us about Human Diversity," in Fox, S.W. (ed.): *Individuality and Determinism* (New York, 1984).
18. --------, Heston, L.L., Eckert, E., Keyes, M., and Resnick, S.: "The Minnesota Study of Twins Reared Apart: Project Description and Sample Results in the Developmental Domain," in Gedda, L., Parisi, P., and Nance, W.E. (eds.): *Twin Research 3. Intelligence, Personality and Development*, pp. 227-233 (New York, 1981).
19. Burlingham, D.: *Twins: A Study of Three Pairs of Identical Twins* (New York, 1952).
20. Campion, E., and Tucker, G.: "A Note on Twin Studies, Schizophrenia, and Neurological Impairment," *Archives of General Psychiatry*, v. 29, p. 460 (1973).
21. Carter, C.O.: "An ABC of Medical Genetics. VI – Polygenic Inheritance and Common Diseases," *Lancet*, v. 1, p. 1253 (1969).
22. --------, and Evans, K.A.: "Inheritance of Congenital Pyloric Stenosis," *Journal of Medical Genetics*, v. 6, p. 233 (1969).
23. Cohen, D.J., Dibble, E., Grawe, J.M. et al.: "Separating Identical from Fraternal Twins," *Archives of General Psychiatry*, v. 29, p. 465 (1973).
24. Dank, B.M.: "Six Homosexual Siblings," *Archives of Sexual Behavior*, v. 1, p. 193 (1971).
25. Darke, R.: "Heredity as an Etiological Factor in Homosexuality," *The Journal of Nervous and Mental Disease*, v. 107, p. 251 (1948).
25A. Darke, R.: "Homosexual Activity," *The Journal of Nervous and Mental Disease*, v. 108, p. 217 (1948).
26. Darlington, C. D.: "Heredity and Environment," *Caryologia Suppl.*, v. 6, p. 370 (1954).

27. Davison, K., Brierly, H., and Smith, C.: "A Male Monozygotic Twinship Discordant for Homosexuality," *British Journal of Psychiatry*, v. 118, p. 675 (1971).

28. Dawkins, R.: *The Selfish Gene* (Oxford, 1976).

29. Devereux, G.: "Institutionalized Homosexuality of the Mohave Indians," *Human Biology*, v. 9, p. 489 (1937).

30. Dobzhansky, T., Ayala, F.J., Stebbins, G.L., and Valentine, D.W.: *Evolution* (San Francisco, 1977).

31. Dukes, C. E.: "Genetics in Relation to Surgery," *Ann. Roy. Coll. Surg. Engl.*, v. 28, p. 1 (1961).

32. East, W.N.: "Sexual Offenders," *Journal of Nervous and Mental Disease*, v. 103, p. 626 (1946).

32A. Eckert, E.D., Bouchard, T.J., Bohlen, J. and Heston, L.L.: "Homosexuality in Monozygotic Twins Reared Apart," *British Journal of Psychiatry*, v. 148, p. 421 (1985). Reprinted here.

33. Essen-Moller, E.: "Twin Research in Psychiatry," *Acta Psychiat. Scand.*, v. 39, p. 65 (1963).

34. Farber, S.: *Identical Twins Raised Apart* (New York, 1981).

35. Fenichel, O.: *The Psychoanalytic Theory of Neurosis* (New York, 1945).

36. Feibleman, J.K.: "The Role of Hypotheses in the Scientific Method," *Perspectives Med. & Biol.*, v. 2, p. 335 (1959).

37. Fischbein, S.: "Onset of Puberty in MZ and DZ Twins," *Acta Geneticæ Medicæ et Gemellogiæ*, v. 27, p. 151 (1977).

38. Freud, S.: *Three Essays on the Theory of Sexuality* (London, 1949).

39. --------: "Psychoanalytic Notes upon an Autobiographical Account of a Case of Paranoia," in *The Standard Edition of the Complete Psychological Works*, v. 12 (London, 1948).

40. Friedman, R.C., Wolleson, F., and Tendler, R.: "Psychological Development and Levels of Sex Steroids in Male Identical Twins of Divergent Sexual Orientation," *Journal of Nervous and Mental Disease*, v. 163, p. 282 (1976).

41. Gates, R. R.: *Human Genetics* (New York, 1946).

42. Gedda, L., and Brenci, G.: "Twins as a Natural Test of Chronogenetics," *Acta Geneticæ Medicæ et Gemellogiæ*, v. 24, p. 15 (1975).

43. Gladue, B.A., Green, R. and Hellman, R.E.: "Neuroendocrine Response to Estrogen and Sexual Orientation," *Science*, v. 225, p. 1496 (1984).
44. Glass, S.F., Denel, H.F., and Wright, C.A.: "Sex Hormone Studies in Male Homosexuality," *Endocrinology*, v. 26, p. 590 (1940).
45. Goldschmidt, R.: *Physiological Genetics* (New York, 1938).
46. Gottesman, I. and Carey, G.: "Extracting Meaning and Information from Twin Data," *Psychiatric Developments*, v. 1, p. 35 (1983).
47. Gottesman, I.I., and Shields, J.: "Schizophrenia in Twins: 16 Years' Consecutive Admissions to a Psychiatric Clinic," *British Journal of Psychiatry*, v. 112, p. 809 (1966).
48. Green, R.: *Sexual Identity Conflict in Children and Adolescents*, pp. 141-90 (New York, 1974).
49. --------, and Money, J.: "Incongruous Gender Role: Nongenital Manifestations in Prepubertal Boys," *The Journal of Nervous and Mental Disease*, v. 131, p. 160 (1960).
50. --------, and Stoller, R.J.: "Two Monozygotic (Identical) Twin Pairs Discordant for Homosexuality," *Archives of Sexual Behavior*, v. 1, p. 321 (1971).
51. Grumbach, M.M. and Barr, M.L.: "Cytologic Tests of Chromosomal Sex in Relation to Sexual Anomalies in Man," in *Recent Progress in Hormone Research*, v. 14 (New York, 1958).
52. Habel, H.: "Zwillingsuntersuchungen an Homosexuellen," *Zeitschrift für Sexualforschung*, v. 1, p. 161 (1950).
53. Hamilton, W.D.: "The Genetical Theory of Social Behavior. I.," *Journal of Theoretical Biology*, v. 7, pp. 1-16 (1964).
54. Hamilton, W.D.: "The Genetical Theory of Social Behavior. II.," *Journal of Theoretical Biology*, v. 7, pp. 17-32 (1964).
55. Hampshire, S.: "The Illusion of Sociobiology," *New York Review of Books*, pp. 64-69, October 12, 1978.
56. Hare, E.H. (ed.): *The Bethlehem Royal Hospital and the Maudsley Hospital Triennial Statistical Report, Years 1958-1960*, London: The Bethlehem Royal Hospital and the Maudsley Hospital (1962).
57. Harris, H.: "Inherited Variations of Human Plasma Proteins," *Brit Med Bull*, v. 17, p. 217 (1961).

58. Harris, H. and Kallmus, H.: "Measurement of Taste Sensitivity to Phenylthiourea (P. T. C.)," *Ann. Eugenics*, v. 15, p. 24 (1949).
59. Henderson, G.D. and Gillespie, R.D.: *Textbook of Psychiatry for Students and Practitioners* (London, 1946).
60. Henry, G.W.: *Sex Variants* (New York, 1948).
61. Heston, L.L., and Shields, J.: "Homosexuality in Twins. A Family Study and a Registry Study," *Archives of General Psychiatry*, v. 18, p. 149 (1968). Reprinted here.
62. Hilton, B., Callahan, D., Harris, M., Condliffe, P., and Berkley, B.: *Ethical Issues in Human Genetics* (New York, 1973).
63. Hirschfeld, M.: *Sexualpathologie* (Bonn, 1916 and 1921).
64. -------- : *Die Homosexualität des Mannes und des Weibes* (Berlin, 1920).
65. -------- : *Sexual Pathology* (New York, 1940).
66. Hoch, P.H. and Zubin, J.: *Psychosexual Development in Health and Disease* (New York, 1949).
67. Holeman, R.E., and Winokur, G.: "Effeminate Homosexuality: A Disease of Childhood," *Amer J Orthopsychiat*, v. 35, p. 48 (1965).
68. Holt, S.B.: *The Genetics of Dermal Ridges*, pp. 80-81 (Springfield, 1968).
69. Hrubec, Z. and Robinette, C.D.: "The Study of Human Twins in Medical Research," *New England Journal of Medicine*, v. 310, p. 435 (1984).
70. Hull, D.L.: *Philosophy of Biological Science* (Englewood Cliffs, 1974).
71. --------: "The Trouble with Traits," *Theory and Decision* (1978).
72. Hutchinson, G.E.: "A Speculative Consideration of Certain Possible Forms of Sexual Selection in Man," *American Naturalist*, v. 93, p. 81 (1959).
73. Jensch, K.: "Zur Genealogie der Homosexualität," *Arch. Psychiat. Berl.*, v. 112, p. 527 (1941).
74. -------- : "Weiterer Beitrag zur Genealogie der Homosexualität," *Arch. Psychiat. Berl.*, v. 112, p. 679 (1941).
75. Kallmann, F.J.: "Comparative Twin Study on the Genetic Aspects of Male Homosexuality," *The Journal of Nervous and Mental Disease*, v. 115, p. 283 (1952). Reprinted here.

76. -------- : "The Use of Genetics in Psychiatry," *J. Ment. Sc.*, v. 104, p. 542 (1952).

77. -------- : "Twin and Sibship Study of Overt Male Homosexuality," *Amer. J. Hum. Genet.*, v. 4, p. 136 (1952).

78. -------- : *Heredity in Health and Mental Disorder*, pp. 116-119 (New York, 1953).

79. Kallmann, F.J. and Anastasio,M.: "Twin Studies on the Psychopathology of Suicide," *The Journal of Nervous and Mental Disease*, v. 105, p. 40 (1947).

80. Kallmann, F.J., DePorte, J., DePorte, E., and Feingold, L.: "Suicide in Twins and Only Children," *The American Journal of Human Genetics*, v. 1, p. 113 (1949).

81. Kinsey, A.C., Pomeroy, W.B., and Martin, C.E.: *Sexual Behavior in the Human Male* (Philadelphia and London, 1948).

82. Klintworth, G.K.: "A Pair of Male Monozygotic Twins Discordant for Homosexuality," *Journal of Nervous and Mental Disease*, v. 135, p. 113 (1962). Reprinted here.

83. Koch, G.: "Die Bedeutung genetischer Faktoren für das menschliche Verhalten," *Ärzliche Praxis*, v. 17, pp. 823 and 839-846 (1965).

84. Kolb, L.C. and Johnson, A.M.: "Etiology and Therapy of Overt Homosexuality," *Psychoanalyt. Quart.*, v. 24, p. 506 (1955).

85. Koller, S.: "Über die Andwendbarkeit und Verbesserung der Probandenmethode. Schlusswort zu den Bemerkungen von Th. Lang," *Ztschr. menschl. Vereb.*, v. 26, p. 444 (1942).

86. Krafft-Ebing, R.: *Psychopathia Sexualis* (New York, 1922; Stuttgart, 1924).

87. Lang, T.: "Beitrag zur Frage nach der genetischen Bedingheit der Homosexualität," *Ztschr. ges. Neurol. Psychiat.*, v. 155, p. 702 (1936).

88. -------- : "Weiterer Beitrag zur Frage nach der genetischen Bedingtheit der Homosexualität," *Ztschr. ges. Neurol. Psychiat.*, v. 162, p. 627 (1938).

89. -------- : "Vierter Beitrag zur Frage nach der genetischen Bedingtheit der Homosexualität," *Ztschr. ges. Neurol. Psychiat.*, v. 166, p. 255 (1939).

90. -------- : "Studies on the Genetic Determination of Homosexuality," *The Journal of Nervous and Mental Disease*, v. 92, p. 55, 1940.

91. -------- : "Beitrag zur Frage nach dem Verkommen einer totalen fütalen Geschlechtsumwandlung beim Menschen," *Arch. Julius Klaus Stift.*, v. 19, p. 45 (1944).

92. -------- : "Zur Frage nach der genetischen Struktur von Homsexuellen und deren Eltern," *Arch. Julius Klaus Stift.*, v. 20, p. 51 (1945).

93. Lange, J.: *Crime as Destiny: A Study of Criminal Twins*, pp. 154-160 (London, 1931). Originally published as *Verbrechen als Shicksal: Studien an kriminellen Zwillingen* (Leipzig, 1929).

94. Lerner, I.M.: *The Genetic Basis of Selection* (New York, 1958).

95. Lewontin, R.C.: *The Genetic Basis of Evolutionary Change* (New York, 1974).

96. Lidz, T., Schafer, S., Cornelison, A., and Terry, D.: "Ego Differentiation and Schizophrenic Symptom Formation in Identical Twins," *J Amer Psychoanal Assoc*, v. 10, p. 74 (1962).

97. London, L.S. and Caprio, F.S.: *Sexual Deviations* (Washington, 1950).

98. Marmor, J.: *Sexual Inversion: the Multiple Roots of Homosexuality* (New York, 1965).

99. Mattis, S., French, J.H., and Rapin, R.: "Dyslexia in Children and Young Adults: Three Independent Neuropsychological Syndromes," *Dev Med Child Neurol*, v. 17, p. 150 (1975).

100. McConaghy, N.: "Penile Volume Change to Moving Pictures of Male and Female Nudes in Heterosexual and Homosexual Males," *Behav Res Ther*, v. 5, p. 43 (1967).

101. --------: "Aversive and Positive Conditioning Treatments of Homosexuality," *Behav Res Ther*, v. 13, p. 309 (1975).

102. --------: "Is a Homosexual Orientation Irreversible?" *British Journal of Psychiatry*, v. 129, p. 556 (1976).

103. --------, Armstrong, M.S., Birrell, P.C., and Buhrich, N.: "The Incidence of Bisexual Feelings and Opposite Sex Behavior in Medical Students," *Journal of Nervous and Mental Disease*, v. 67, p. 685 (1979).

104. -------- and Blaszczynski, A.: "A Pair of Monozygotic Twins Discordant for Homosexuality: Sex-Dimorphic Behavior and

Penile Volume Responses," *Archives of Sexual Behavior,* v. 9, p. 127 (1980). Reprinted here.

105. Mead, M.: *Male and Female* (New York, 1949).

106. Medawar, P. B.: "The Homograft Reaction," *Proc. Roy. Soc. [Biol.],* v. 149, p. 145 (1958).

107. -------- : *The Uniqueness of the Individual,* pp. 150-152 (London, 1957).

108. Mitchell, M. B. and Mitchell, H. K.: "A Case of 'Maternal' Inheritance in *Neurospora crassa,*" *Proc. Nat. Acad. Sci. U.S.A.,* v. 38, p. 442 (1952).

109. Money, J., Hampson, J.G. and Hampson, J.L.:"Hermaphroditism: Recommendations Concerning Assignment of Sex, Change of Sex, and Psychologic Management," *Bull. Johns Hopkins Hosp.,* v. 97, p. 284 (1955).

110. --------, --------, and -------- : "An Examination of Some Basic Sexual Concepts: The Evidence of Human Hermaphroditism," *Bull. Johns Hopkins Hosp.,* v. 97, p. 301 (1955).

111. -------- : "Factors in the Genesis of Homosexuality," in Winokur, G. (ed.): *Determinants of Sexual Behavior* (Springfield, 1962).

112. -------- : "Genetic and Chromosomal Aspects of Homosexual Etiology," in Marmor,J. (ed.): *Homosexual Behavior: A Modern Reappraisal,* pp. 59-72 (New York, 1980).

113. Moore, K.L. and Barr, M.L.: "Smears from the Oral Mucosa in the Detection of Chromosomal Sex," *Lancet,* v. 2, p. 57 (1955).

113A. --------: "Sex Reversal in Newborn Babies," *The Lancet,* v. 1, p. 217 (1959).

114. Morris, S.: "Darwin and the Double Standard," *Playboy,* p. 108 (August, 1978).

115. Myers, M.F.: "Homosexuality, Sexual Dysfunction, and Incest in Male Identical Twins," *Canadian Journal of Psychiatry,* v. 27, p. 144 (1982).

116. Nanney, D. L.: "The Role of Cytoplasm in Heredity," in McElroy, W. D. and Glass, B.: *Chemical Basis of Heredity,* pp. 134-164 (Baltimore, 1957).

117. Nixon, W.L.B.: "On the Diagnosis of Twin-Pair Ovularity and the use of Dermatoglyphic Data," in Gedda, L.: *Novant' Anni delle Leggi Mendeliane,* pp. 235-45 (Rome, 1956).

118. Oster, C.F. and Wilson, E.O.: *Caste and Ecology in the Social Insects* (Princeton, 1978).
119. Pare, C.M.B.: "Homosexuality and Chromosomal Sex," *Journal of Psychosomatic Research*, v. 1, p. 247 (1956).
120. Paluszny, M., and Abelson, A.G.: "Twins in a Child Psychiatry Clinic," *American Journal of Psychiatry*, v. 132, p. 434 (1975).
121. Parker, N.: "Homosexuality in Twins: A Report on Three Discordant Pairs," *British Journal of Psychiatry*, v. 110, p. 489 (1964).
122. -------- : "Twins: A Psychiatric Study of a Neurotic Group," *Med J Aust*, v. 2, p. 735 (1964).
123. Pollin, W., Stabeneau, J.R., and Tupin, J.: "Family Studies with Identical Twins Discordant for Schizophrenia," *Psychiatry*, v. 28, p. 60 (1965).
124. Price, J.: "Human Polymorphism," *J Med Genet*, v. 4, p. 44 (1967).
125. Raboch, J. and Nedoma, K.: "Sex Chromatin and Sexual Behavior," *Psychosomatic Medicine*, v. 20, p. 55 (1958).
126. Race, R. R. and Sanger, R.: *Blood Groups in Man*, pp. 296-302 (Oxford, 1958).
127. Rainer, J. D. and Kallmann, F. J.: "The Role of Genetics in Psychiatry," *The Journal of Nervous and Mental Disease*, v. 126, p. 403 (1958).
128. Rainer, J. D., Mesnikoff, A., Kolb, L. C. and Carr, A.: "Homosexuality and Heterosexuality in Identical Twins," *Psychosomatic Medicine*, v. 22, p. 251 (1960). Reprinted here.
129. Reinish, J.M.: "Fetal Hormones, the Brain, and Human Sex Differences," *Archives of Sexual Behavior*, v. 3, p. 51 (1974).
130. Ruse, M.: *The Philosophy of Biology* (London, 1973).
131. --------: "Sociobiology: Sound Science or Muddled Metaphysics?" in Suppe, F. and Asquith, P. (eds.): *PSA 1976*, vol. 2, Lansing, MI: Philosophy of Science Association.
132. --------: *Sociobiology: Sense or Nonsense?* (Dordrecht, 1979).
133. --------: "Are There Gay Genes? Sociobiology and Homosexuality," *The Journal of Homosexuality*, v. 6, p. 5 (1981). Reprinted here.
134. Sanders, J.: "Homosexual Twillinge," *Genetica*, v. 16, p. 401 (1934).

135. -------- : "Homosexual Twins," *Ned. Teschr. Geneesk.*, v. 78, p. 3346 (1934).

136. Schilder, P.: "Über Identifizierung aud Grund der Analyse eines Falles von Homosexualität," *Ztschr. ges. Neurol. Psychiat.*, v. 59, p. 217 (1920).

137. Shields, J.: "Psychiatric Genetics" in Shepherd, M. and Davies, D.L. (eds.): *Studies in Psychiatry*, London (no date given).

138. -------- : *Monozygotic Twins Brought up Apart and Brought up Together* (London, 1962).

139. -------- , and Slater, E.: "La Similarité du Diagnostic chez les Jumeaux et le Problème de la Spécificité Biologique dans les Névroses et les Troubles de la Personnalité," *Evolut Psychiat*, v. 31, p. 441 (1966).

140. Siegelman, M.: "Birth Order and Family Size of Homosexual Men and Women," *Journal of Consulting and Clinical Psychology*, v. 41, p.164 (1973).

141. Slater, E.: "The Genetical Aspects of Personality and Neurosis," *Congrès International de Psychiatrie*, v. VI (Paris, 1950).

142. -------- : "Birth Order and Maternal Age of Homosexuals," *The Lancet*, v. 1, p. 69 (1962).

143. -------- : "Diagnosis of Zygosity by Fingerprints," *Acta Psychiat*, v. 39, p. 78 (1963).

144. -------- , with the assistance of Shields, J.: *Psychotic and Neurotic Illness in Twins*, Medical Research Council Special Report Series No. 278, Her Majesty's Stationery Office (1953).

145. -------- : Personal communication to Klintworth, 1960.

146. Smith, S.M. and Penrose, L.S.: "Monozygotic and Dizygotic Twin Diagnosis," *Ann. Human Genetics*, v. 19, p. 273 (1954-55).

147. Sonneborn, T. M.: "The Cytoplasm in Heredity," *Heredity*, v. 4, p. 11 (1950).

148. Spiro, C.: As quoted by Sanders, J. in "Homosexual Twillinge," *Genetica*, v. 16, p. 401 (1934).

149. Stern, C: *Principles of Human Genetics* (San Francisco, 1949; 3rd edition 1973).

149A. Stoller, A.: "Sexual Deviation in the Male," *Med Press*, v. 216, p. 262 (1946).

150. Strickberger, M.W.: *Genetics* (New York, 1968).

151. Sullivan, H.S.: *The Interpersonal Theory of Psychiatry*, Perry, H.S. and Carvel, M.L. (eds.), (New York, 1953).
152. Symons, D.: *The Evolution of Human Sexuality* (New York, 1979).
153. Terman, L. M., Miles, C. C. *et al.*: *Sex and Personality*, pp. 1-600 (London, 1936).
154. Tienari, P: "On Intrapair Differences in Male Twins with Special Reference to Dominance-Submissiveness," *Acta Psychiat*, suppl 188 (1966).
155. Tripp, C.A.: *The Homosexual Matrix* (New York, 1975).
156. Trivers, R.L.: "Parent-offspring conflict," *American Zoologist*, v. 14, p. 249 (1974).
157. -------- and Willard, D.E.: "Natural Selection of Parental Ability to Vary the Sex Ratio of Offspring," *Science*, v. 179, p. 90 (1973).
158. Waddington, C.H.: *The Strategy of the Genes* (London, 1957).
159. Wagner, R. P. and Mitchell, H. K.: *Genetics and Metabolism*, pp. 312-343 (New York, 1955).
160. Ward, I.L.: "Prenatal Stress Feminizes and Demasculinizes the Behavior of Males," *Science*, v.175, p. 82 (1972).
161. Weinrich, J.D.: *Human Reproductive Strategy. I. Environmental Predictability and Reproductive Strategy; Effects of Social Class and Race. II. Homosexuality and Non-reproduction; Some Evolutionary Models.* Unpublished doctoral dissertation, Harvard University, 1976.
162. West, D. J.: *Homosexuality*, pp. 1-200 (Penguin Books, Middlesex, 1960).
163. Wiener, A.S., and Leff, I.L.: "Chances of Establishing Non-Identity of Binovular Twins with Special Reference to Individuality Tests of the Blood," *Genetics*, v. 25, p. 197 (1940).
164. Williams, G.C.: *Adaptation and Natural Selection: A Critique of Some Current Evolutionary Thought* (Princeton, 1966).
165. Wilson, E.O.: "Human decency is animal," *The New York Times Magazine*, pp. 38-50 , October 12, 1975.
166. --------: *Sociobiology: The New Synthesis* (Cambridge, 1975).
167. --------: *On Human Nature* (Cambridge, 1978).

168. Wilson, R.S., Brown, A.M., and Matheny, A.P., Jr.: "Emergence and Persistence of Behavioral Differences in Twins," *Child Development*, v. 42, p. 1381 (1971).
169. --------: "Blood Typing and Twin Zygosity," *Human Heredity*, v. 20, p. 30 (1970).
170. World Health Organization: "The Use of Twins in Epidemiological Studies," *Acta Genetica*, v. 15, p. 109 (1966).
171. Zuger, B.: "Effeminate Behavior Present in Boys from Early Childhood: I. The Clinical Syndrome and Follow-up Studies," *Jour Pediatr*, v. 69, p. 1098 (1966).
172. --------: "The Role of Familial Factors in Persistent Effeminate Behavior in Boys," *American Journal of Psychiatry*, v. 126, p. 151 (1970).
173. --------: "Monozygotic Twins Discordant for Homosexuality: Report of a Pair and Significance of the Phenomenon," *Comprehensive Psychiatry*, v. 17, p. 661 (1976). Reprinted here.